PAPER COLLAGE
CHINESE STYLE
Zhu Liqun Paper Arts Museum

PAPER COLLAGE
CHINESE STYLE
Zhu Liqun Paper Arts Museum

Better Link Press

On page 1
Buddhist Temple Secreted in Blossoming Flowers
Paper: embossed paper
Dimensions: 25 × 25 cm
This paper collage is a sister piece of *The Winding Path to the Secluded Place* (see page 56) in our lessons. The work generalizes and transforms the temple, path, flowers and trees with freehand brush style, portraying a scene of ethereality and calmness.

On pages 2–3
Returning of the Wild Geese
Paper: cardstock, embossed paper, printing paper, and mulberry paper
Dimensions: 30 × 21 cm
This collage was created when the author discovered a new type of paper. The mulberry paper has a flocculent texture which is perfect for representing flourishing woods. Meanwhile, the brownish background, greenish leaves, explicit birds and trunks are perfectly mingled together to conclude this piece of art, presenting a unique art style like a delicate artistic rug.

This book is edited and designed by the Editorial Committee of *Cultural China* series

For Zhu Liqun Paper Arts Museum
Project Designers: Zhu Liqun, Yao Xiaoyan
Text and Photographs: Wang Chenbo
Works: Zhu Liqun, Yao Xiaoyan, Liu Xiuxia, Wang Chenbo, Zhu Jiayan, Qian Ciying, Yan Wenjun, Qian Caidi, Ji Yunting, Chen Xinyi, Li Liwen, Zhang Danyi, Zhang Keqing, Hu Weiyuan, Yang Ningyuan, Yin Zhiren, Tang Ge, Tang Shi, Dai Yuming, Qian Ruoyan, Ding Jianing, Hu Junhao, Wen Yanbo, Tang Hongwen, Yu Xinyue.
Technique Demonstration: Liu Xiuxia

Translation: Kitty Lau
Cover Design: Wang Wei
Interior Design: Li Jing, Hu Bin (Yuan Yinchang Design Studio)

Editor: Wu Yuezhou
Editorial Director: Zhang Yicong

Senior Consultants: Sun Yong, Wu Ying, Yang Xinci
Managing Director and Publisher: Wang Youbu

ISBN: 978-1-60220-023-4

Address any comments about *Paper Collage: Chinese Style* to:

Better Link Press
99 Park Ave
New York, NY 10016
USA

or

Shanghai Press and Publishing Development Company, Ltd.
F 7 Donghu Road, Shanghai, China (200031)
Email: comments_betterlinkpress@hotmail.com

Printed in China by Shenzhen Donnelley Printing Co., Ltd.
1   3   5   7   9   10   8   6   4   2

CONTENTS

Above
Prawns
Paper: embossed paper, tracing paper, and sketch paper
Dimensions: 20 × 20 cm
With the reference of *Prawns* by Qi Baishi (1864–1957), an influential Chinese painter, this collage is illustrated by various shades of gray paper to simulate the various tonality of Chinese painting. The composition and assembling of paper pieces thoroughly reflect the texture and form of prawn. Although there is a lot of empty space on the background, the picture of two prawns swimming in a river are vividly presented.

CONTENTS

Bottom
Flowers in a Vase (Realism)
Paper: embossed paper, printing paper, and sketch paper
Dimensions: 54 × 39 cm
Realism is an artistic presentation style characterized by actual representation of the subjects, often contrasted with freehand brush style. Although freehand brush style is more appropriate for paper collage making, it does not mean that realism cannot be achieved. This collage is successfully composed in realism style by skillfully overlapping paper pieces of the same shades, carefully capturing the subject features, and intricately demonstrating the relationship between light and shadow.

Facing page
Sunset
Paper: embossed paper and printing paper
Dimensions: 25 × 25 cm
This collage is fabricated with large pieces as the background and small pieces as the embellishment to display the twilight scene over the ocean. The composition and assembling are very simple and yet vividly demonstrate the layering effect through the diverse colors.

INTRODUCTION

The art of paper collage started when a three-year-old girl who did something unintentionally. Tearing a piece of paper that changes its shape is an act of destruction in the eyes of an adult who has lots of knowledge and regulations. To a child with a great deal of curiosity, it, however, brings tremendous joy. This is the natural impulsive reaction towards transformation. We even think that all kinds of art are developed from this kind of childlike instinct.

The little girl was not scolded because of her "destruction." She, therefore, paid more attention on paper tearing and produced lots of torn pieces scattered all around. All of a sudden, she held up a scrap and said, "This is a bird." My original plan was just sitting next to her, observing her cuteness, and experiencing her joy. However, this "bird" aroused my sense of art that pushed me to generate an actual artistic creation.

"Is this bird flying?"

"Yes!"

"Then it should have a pair of spread wings."

The little girl thought for a moment, torn out a smaller piece, and placed it on the shoulder of the bird. "The bird should have a buddy." "There should be some clouds in the sky." I brought out some suggestions to stimulate her brain power and she started to think herself. We were like two artists developing a joyful scene of paper collage. I tried my best to dig out all kinds of paper in different colors and materials. At the same time, I restrained myself from putting my hands to it. Seeing her as a tutor, like Pablo Picasso, with respect, I neglected the rule of proportion and perspective and let her freely arrange the collage. Upon receiving her permission, I would help her glue. If my work, however, was not satisfying, I would ask her

Facing page
The Watertown
Paper: embossed paper, printing paper, and sketch paper
Dimensions: 21 × 30 cm
This artwork uses a new collage technique—scraping. A knife is used to scrape off partial of the paper that is glued on the background so that the remaining portion becomes translucent to simulate the watercolor brushstroke. The greenish paper is selected to present vegetation while the black and white paper is integrated to build the roofs and walls, displaying a unique scene of water towns in Jiangnan region of China.

Daisies
Paper: tissue, embossed paper, printing paper, and sketch paper
Dimensions: 54 × 39 cm
This collage is composed of cold colors, using large pieces for the background and white pieces for the daisies. The use of soft tissue paper creates a fresh and vague scene just like an impressionist painting.

to correct me. She was sometimes exciting, sometimes contemplating. Finally, we completed our first creative art. (Or I should say accompanied her to finish the art.) The artwork was naive and yet lively. From that point on, paper collage became her impulsive reaction of creating and venting; and I was invited every time. The mind of the three-year-old was filled with living birds, kittens, giant pandas, dolphins, flowers … She started to think about putting the moon on the dark blue paper and light yellow shadows around the clouds. She even consciously tore out different features to distinguish the giant panda from dolphin.

The little girl was full of fascination when dealing with the scraps to create a piece of art, from the fortuitous imagination to the valiant attempt. Our paper collage creative team was established in the same way. All these years, we have demanded ourselves to be like the little girl, having the valiant imagination that can fire up our creativity. At the same time, we actively review the unexpected outcomes from our design process, which we can gain more creativity and imagination. The key of paper collage making is to discover our power of imagination. Without it, the art will become mechanical and boring no matter how great the techniques and theories that we have.

1. New Type of Art

Paper collage has become a new type of art due to the rapid growth in industrialization. The modern technology encourages new design concepts and artistic ideas, breaking away from the traditional practice. The development of paper industry provides a great variety of paper material, in terms of function, texture, color, that improves our business, economy, science, culture, and way of living. The wide range of thickness, density, stiffness, and texture combining with different techniques deliver an amazing presentation. When we start tearing, the differences will appear and we can experience the unexpected changes. The crumpled and faded paper that we are about to throw away is now a makeover through paper collage processing. Every torn piece is different. There is no identical torn piece: different direction of tearing exposes different texture effect, tracing paper being glued on different background creates different color effect, and different paper weight and density determines different tearing effects. These variations are quite interesting as long as we have enough preparation and are willing to utilize the differences and changes, making paper collage full of fun and diversity.

2. Fundamental Concept

Our philosophy and concept of creative paper collage is based on the traditional Chinese painting. In this book, you will find the references to "scatter perspective"—a unique Chinese paining technique, as well as the technical use of wet painting brush, from dark to light, to finish in one go from simply one dot. You will also learn how the traditional Chinese painters prepare their state of mind, having a well-thought-out plan and complete with a great confidence. The style of paper collage is similar to the freehand brush technique of Chinese painting. It concentrates on loose and unconstrained style to fully express sentiments rather than realistic presentation or technical details. Through the works of paper collage and the artists' unlimited imaginations, you will be able to realize their concepts and messages.

The charisma of art is derived from variations. No matter it is music, dance or art, it will deteriorate or vanish without variations. Same as other types of art, the charisma of paper collage is depended on variations. In the exploration process, its art styles, presentation methods, and technical skills are continuously changing, producing certain amount of uncertainties. In fact, the attractiveness of paper collage is extracted from the process of capturing, following, and creating the changes.

The Woods
Paper: embossed paper and sketch paper
Dimensions: 54 × 25 cm
The technique of cutting is widely used in this collage to fabricate the trees, showing the slim, upright, and neat trunks. Other components are constructed by using the technique of tearing in order to exhibit the casual and free style. When the two styles are integrated together, a strong comparison is developed forming a unique artistic beauty.

The Lotus
Paper: cardstock, embossed paper and tracing paper
Dimensions: 20 × 20 cm
This collage refers to the composition of lotus in traditional Chinese painting—using grayish shades to portray the different values of the stems and red to illustrate the lotus flower which highlights the picture as well as the theme. In addition, the translucent tracing paper perfectly renders the beauty of the mist.

3. Self-Exploration

Going through creating paper collage can help you become more confident.

The artists from this book includes elementary school kids, middle and high school students, professionals from all areas as well as artists in their 60's. A lot of them were new to paper collage. Through interacting with paper, learning and creating, they were attracted by the variations of paper collage. When they first started, they were confused and lost when encountering the changes. Later on, however, they actively seek for changes, and eventually created many new techniques and gained the sense of accomplishment.

This is an art that allows you to express your own self whether it is naive, experienced, general, exaggerated, deformed, conceptual or abstract. A paper collage can be a gift as well as a home decoration. You can go very deep to explore one theme and very wild to express your thoughts. Due to the uniqueness of its materials and techniques, paper collage is not as detailed as oil painting but you can make use of the assembling of scraps, changes of texture, and variations of styles to express an exceptional effect that other types of art cannot achieve. The art of paper collage is very sentimental and self-concentrated. It requires techniques and certain level of cultivation; but the most important of all is to get your hands dirty and work confidently. We should act like the little girl, switching on the imagination mode and elevating the potential to vitality. Every paper collage lover can become an incomparable artist.

We suggest following the lessons to get familiar with paper collage and yet do not overcautiously interprets every step as the absolute authority. Naturally adapt to the differences and variations. Give yourself more room for elaboration and continuously improve yourself, in which you can create your own art piece as the biggest reward.

The Girl
Paper: cardstock and magazine paper
Dimensions: 30 × 60 cm
This girl with an origami crane in her hands is developed by selecting images from magazines. Her facial features, clothes, and hands are very much true to life and properly displayed under a natural lighting effect. The green crane, delicately crafted, looks three-dimensional and lifelike. This kind of realism art, similar to a photograph, is not commonly found in this book.

CHAPTER ONE
The Art of Paper Collage

As implied by the name, paper collage is an assemblage of paper in different sizes, forms, and colors through gluing to create an art. The varying paper pieces are like the brushwork of oil painting with the exception that the colors of paper pieces cannot be completely blended as oil paints. This causes some limitations; on the other hand, this generates unique qualities: brisk, enthusiastic, and decorative.

1. The Basics: Imagination and Creativity

Before this chapter, we have talked about the creation process of a three-year-old girl in the Introduction. This illustrates that creativity is often initiated by random imagination and is active throughout the whole process. The little girl does not have what we call the acquired "artistic quality" but she has the common potential imagination. The association of the paper piece with the "bird" is random; however, the making of the wings is spontaneous and bold. She also relates her joyful heart with various colors to create the "colorful clouds" all over the sky. The trees and lawn are torn pieces. If one piece is not enough, she assembles together several pieces in various sizes. Although she has not learned the techniques of paper collage, she incredibly demonstrates the mightiness of imagination.

Imagination is the ability of mind associating two or more items to create new ideas. A lot of Chinese idioms are derived from imagination: "the thing reminds one of its owner" (associating an item with a person); and "imagination flashes like flying birds" (associating lots of unrelated items). This ability of mind lives in everyone. When imagination meets with creative ideas, it initiates a series of target-oriented spontaneous actions. This is creation.

Facing page
The Landscape
Paper: embossed paper, printing paper, and sketch paper
Dimensions: 39 × 54 cm
This collage is constructed by various techniques such as folding, crumpling, pinching, and splitting, transforming the two-dimensional paper to three-dimensional artwork, strongly presenting the relief art form. The overlapping paper truly presents the magnificent scene of continuous mountain ranges.

The Moon Rises above the Sea
Paper: embossed paper and cardstock
Dimensions: 30 × 21 cm
The use of splitting technique exposes the fiber of the cardstock to create the waves. The black color emphasizes the atmosphere of the sea at night while the three blue waves strengthen the feature of sea. The moon rising above the sea gives a little punch to the serene sea, performing a simple and yet ethereal collage.

Everyone may have a great deal of creativity. It can be feelings towards an inspirational element in our daily life such as evocative scene, meaningful moment or even a romantic corner. After refinement, these bits and pieces can be transformed to a visual art. Creativity can be a new idea of a theme. For instance, love is an everlasting theme but not all artworks about love evoke the emotional resonance. Using a newfangled combination to illustrate love, a big dog with a small bird for example, can develop an innovated idea. Creativity can also be materials and techniques. For instance, crumple a piece of paper to make it more three-dimensional or split a piece of paper to produce a rough texture. Imagination provides a platform for thinking and thinking advances imagination. These two work together will generate unlimited power of creativity.

Adults have lots of experience and thus are restricted by "impossibilities" during creation. Children are lack of experience but relatively easy to throw off the shackles. Their imagination power is much stronger than the adults'. One of the Chinese idioms—Horse and oxen are not related—is an analogy of things that have nothing to do with each other. It, however, omits the fact that creativity usually starts with unrelated matters. If we can train ourselves to elaborate the thinking process, like a child associating two unrelated items—a piece of torn paper with a bird, your reward will be more than an artwork. We, therefore, suggest treating the art of paper collage as a relaxed game that promotes interaction between our brain and muscle.

Paper collage is a new, unrestrained, and interesting art. We will go through the styles, compositions, and color options step by step. Of course, the most important of all is having our imagination and creativity. With these two elements, we can develop our own paper collage language.

The Snow on the Mountaintop
Paper: embossed paper, printing paper, and cardstock
Dimensions: 20 × 20 cm
This collage is created with a large amount of irregular pieces in grayish shades to build up the extensive mountaintop and various color pieces to represent the gullies. The snow on the mountaintop is formed by referring to the traditional Chinese painting technique—leaving empty space. Although the artwork includes only a partial of the view, we can still experience the majesty of the mountains.

2. The Language of Paper Collage

Every art has its own form of presentation or language. Take dancing as an example; it is an integration of body movement and music to develop various dancing styles such as hip-hop, ballet, and tango. They all have their own characteristics. So what kind of language does paper collage own?

Irreproducible Nature
Every piece of paper, after tearing, is in a random form with uncertainty. The same person cannot tear out an identical piece or reproduce an identical collage. Even tearing from the same stack of paper can only produce roughly similar pieces. To complete the lessons in this book, we had to redo the collages. No

Ballerinas
Paper: magazine paper and cardstock
Dimensions: 15 × 25 cm
This paper collage is formed by deconstructing the color images of a magazine for further creation, vividly illustrating a pair of ballerinas lithely and gracefully dancing on the stage under the spot light.

matter how hard we tried, none could be replicated exactly the same as the originals. The deviations are: the new stack of yellow paper had a variation in shade, the shape of the piece had a slight difference, the component could not be pasted at the exact position, and so on. Deviations and variations appear in every step of paper collage making but this is the most entertaining part of all!

Paper has its own "characteristics." They become more obvious when we tear them apart. There are a lot of paper types, such as cardstock, embossed paper, corrugated board, tracing paper, and tissue, which are widely used in different industries, technologies, cultures, and daily living. Even the same piece of paper, tearing vertically or horizontally generates a dissimilar result due to the arrangement of fibers. With these reasons, we should not stick to one type of paper. All types of paper can be utilized. Collecting various materials from kitchens, bathrooms, dining tables, shops, paper factories, newspaper kiosks, laboratories, is a very important preparation. When we bring all types of paper from everywhere, it feels like bringing a group of naughty children back home. The continuous exploration and experiment lead us to discover the diversified characteristics of paper.

Making paper collage is like playing a game with a group of children. If you don't understand them, you will make a lot of mistakes. Once you have figured out their characteristics, they become a group of smart and outstanding children who can participate in your imagination and enlighten your creativity to produce an unexpected result. This is a very interesting process. For instance, you can get a lot of great colors from magazine paper. But when you tear a piece out, you will get a delicate white edge. If you have a flexible mind, the edge is actually a unique outline that you cannot get from a white piece of paper. When you make a beautiful flower, you will get a rough edge around the perimeter of the petal. This happens when you select a piece of thick and tough paper without thinking. If you elaborate on your imagination and change the point of view, this type of paper is most suitable for making fluffy animals. Sometimes, you are not satisfied with a piece glued on the background and you want to remove it so that you can redo. However, after a certain time, a thin layer of glue mark is formed, partially showing the background color. If you pay attention to it, this can be a new creative technique, but it is impossible to reproduce exactly the same.

Paper collage beginners may face a lot of unforeseeable variations in the making process. These variations are actually new discoveries. Some of the collages from this book are created by beginners of all ages. They have developed new techniques with their flexible mind during the construction process. Making paper collage, therefore, does not have to insist on copying the standards. Otherwise, you will be unproductive and make an interesting work boring.

Diverse Themes

Once we get excited about creation, other problems will come along. How can we find creative themes after finishing the lessons? Of course, paper collage provides a wide range of topics, but we need to have the sense of aesthetic and creativity.

First, we can find some elements in our daily life that touch us. For instance, a pot plant at the window, no matter what color it is, can be exciting under the sunlight. A fluffy dog curling up and dozing around your legs becomes particularly peaceful because of your accompany. Sometimes, a bunch of vegetables in the kitchen sink or a basket of fruits on the dining table can be a good still life theme when you pay attention to the delicate forms and bright colors. Depicting a designated object as a theme is appropriate for the paper collage lovers who begin to move from imitative learning to independent creation.

Second, we can extend our limits to the exterior space. You will find that natural scenery is a common art theme and very suitable for paper collage. Natural scenery is ever-changing. Concerning the style, simply the trees have all sorts of postures. Regarding the colors, from spring to winter, the natural colors can be brilliant, tranquil, enthusiastic, warm or even mysterious, which arouse our creativity. We can use our camera to capture the fascinated scenes; many a little makes

Roses
Paper: embossed paper, cardstock, and printing paper
Dimensions: 25 × 25 cm
Making reference to the coloring technique of gouache painting, this collage is composed of large paper pieces in various colors as the flowers and background, using the splitting technique to simulate the heavy brushstroke of gouache painting.

Lotuses in the Breeze
Paper: embossed paper, cardstock, and printing paper
Dimensions: 25 × 25 cm
Referring to the art style and coloring technique of traditional Chinese painting, the ink of this collage is substituted by black and gray paper pieces, whereas the other colors are substituted by color pieces such as pink and green. The perfect integration of dark and light colors presents a picture of fresh lotuses fluttering in the breeze above the pond.

a mickle. We can also get help from others' shots to expand our library.

In addition, we can also reach out to narratives. Every country or culture has its own widespread classical folktales. For instance, the Chinese idiom "Standing by a tree stump waiting for a hare" delivers a message of being hard-working, not to put your hope in randomness, sitting around waiting for luck. In Chinese literature, there are many folktales or idioms such as: "Returning on a stormy night" describes the eagerness of going home to visit family; "A swallow carries mud in its mouth building nest" illustrates a hard-working swallow; "A mother cow licks her calf" talks about the love of a mother; and "A crow feeds its mother" portrays the respect and care for the elderly. All these can be our topics for paper collage.

The diversity of paper collage themes produces a lot of variations in the creation process when interacting with different materials. This stimulates our eagerness of discovery so that we will continue exploring, learning, and looking for breakthroughs.

Freehand Brush Style and Flexibility

As we mentioned in the Introduction part, the theme, concept, philosophy, technique, and style of paper collage are mainly derived from traditional Chinese painting.

Chinese painting can be divided into three categories: figure, bird-and-flower, and landscape. Its style is usually classified as *gongbi* (fine-brush), freehand brush, and *gongbi* with freehand brush. In this book, we have quite a number of projects using the three categories of Chinese painting. Since paper collage has a very freeform style, its presentation is very much like the freehand brush style of Chinese painting. Freehand brush does not require fine brush work but emphasizes on artistic expression. This generates a simple and yet meaningful art style. Same as freehand brush painting, paper collage is unrestrained and lively, perusing not meticulous depiction but artistic concept and sentimental expression.

Chinese painting does not focus on perspective. Paper collage is also unrestrained from space limits, flexibly capturing elements and scenery to present the artist's subjective point of view. The composition of Chinese painting talks about sparse-dense relationship and that of paper collage concentrates on space relativity, reflecting the void and solid. Chinese painting is particular about the five levels of tonality. In paper collage, the ink density is simulated by using different values of gray and black paper pieces. Chinese painting focuses on the original color of the object as the basic color, emphasizing on artistic expression, intention, and enhancement. Paper collage also focuses on original color but is not after the surrounding environment and lighting effect. It sometimes exaggerates the colors to express the artist's emotions and thoughts. Chinese painting tends to relate one's social consciousness to aesthetic sense. Paper collage also leans towards expressing emotions by portraying related objects and surroundings.

Thus, the unrestrained and freehand style of paper collage closely corresponds to Chinese painting. Integrating its techniques can enrich the presentation of paper collage.

Paper collage has its own language but it does not prevent us from integrating with other art styles. This is a way of seeking further development. We can always refer to the languages of other arts such as the transparency of watercolor painting, intensity of oil painting, sturdiness of print, and texture of relief. These can all be the creative ideas for paper collage making. We do not have to worry about losing the uniqueness of paper collage when mixing with other art languages. Actually, fusing various art languages can elevate the presentation, making the techniques of paper collage art more special and abundant.

A good piece of art requires a strong sense of form, color, view, feeling, and concept. For beginners, accomplishing one of them is already a successful try. No matter you are an artist or a fan, as long as you have the courage to keep trying and no fear of failure, you are on the track to success.

The Memory of the Old Alley
Paper: embossed paper, printing paper, and cardstock
Dimensions: 30 × 30 cm
This old alley in *shikumen* (stone warehouse gate) is a kind of traditional Shanghainese architecture. Using a lot of colorful pieces in various shapes, this fascinating scene of Shanghai is produced in an abstract style. Under the moon in the hazy sky, there is a couple in love meeting in the alley, sharing with us a romantic story.

3. Imitative Learning

There are many ways to learn: imitating and copying are the two main ones. These two methods sound similar but actually are quite different. Copying relies on following the specification, trying to accurately duplicate the model. The key is to implement the standard. Meanwhile, imitating relies not on the quality of the object but the artist's subjective perception. Thus, different results will come up, but it leaves room for artistic expressions. As paper collage carries the irreproducible nature, imitative learning is the best method rather than copying.

Imitating is the natural learning method for children. Almost all learning procedures start with imitating. Let's take a look at the laws of children's imitative learning:

a) Children are curious and sensitive. They actively search for and perceive a model.

b) Compare with adults, children pay less attention on the outcomes and follow the instinct.

c) To children, the most important is not caring about accuracy. They tend to go after their perception.

d) Children do have self-correction but it is not the same as following the standard. This kind of correction is a higher level of perceptual expression.

In general, these four laws reflect the strong self-learning ability of children. Children express themselves through imitation and then collect the experience. They base on the model but modify it during the imitating process using their perception. Thus, the imitative process of children actually carries lot of artistic qualities. Most importantly, learning by imitating is very effective but adults tend not to use this method.

We suggest that adults should learn from children and bravely use imitative learning method to master their paper collage skill. Start with imitation to discover the talents, which is the most important of all. If beginners worry about the absence of techniques, they should begin with imitating and forget about copying the standards. In fact, if one is trying to follow his work as the standard for reproduction, he will not be able to meet the "standards." With these reasons, we provide enough lessons for imitation, going from the easy to difficult. The Introductory Lessons are more precise. Not to mislead anyone, the precise lessons are used to perceive the characteristics of paper collage like the children. They are all about tearing and assembling. Simply follow the steps and produce something similar. They do not have to be exact. Just like the warm up exercise before workout, restructure your thinking process after following a few lessons and you will be able to capture the techniques.

Beginners may worry about their artistic literacy. So let's start with imitating. Do not regard artistic literacy as being very complicated. Paper collage is all about style, color, and creativity. These talents are already rooted in you.

We all have the natural instincts to mix colors. The experiences are collected from our daily living, like cooking, dressing, travelling, shopping, and cultural activities. Doing imitative learning through our lessons and applying your color

Flowers in a Vase (Oil Painting Style)
Paper: embossed paper, printing paper, and sketch paper
Dimensions: 54 × 39 cm
Oil painting is the main stream of painting in the western art history. From the collections of this book, various color paper pieces are used to simulate the unique brushstroke, texture, and three-dimensional presentation of oil painting. The paper selection and technique of this collage are very simple but with unique arrangement, this splendid and colorful art is presented like an oil painting.

The Landscape
Paper: embossed paper, printing paper, and sketch paper
Dimensions: 25 × 25 cm
In this paper collage, various shades of green paper is used to illustrate the flourishing woods. With the pink shades of paper, the twilight of sunset is portrayed in gouache painting style. Embellished with two small cottages, a freehand brush style art work is vividly delivered.

perception, you will eventually learn how to release your emotions through colors onto your artworks.

Paper collage lovers may have a problem of forming styles. They may think that their styles are pretty naive. To solve the problem, the best way is through imitation. If you are careful enough, you will find that most of the artworks in this book are related to scenery and still objects. They can be varied, which are very suitable for imitation. Grasping the precise and realistic styles are indeed difficult, but art styles nowadays have been diversified by all sorts of concepts, opinions, approaches, and schools. Even childlike style can be attractive. The external differentiation of the objects is determined by their features.

Once we capture the features, the overall style can be easily modified. This is very appropriate for our imitative learning. If we stick to the standard, we can only achieve below the standard. If you free yourself when following the standard, you may go beyond the standard. Standard is only a guideline but not the utmost level. As a matter of course, going beyond the standard is natural.

Imitating others cannot originate creativity but collect inspirations for future creativity. Creativity may unintentionally enter into your world. It all depends on awareness and "discovery." With no art literacy and techniques, the three-year-old girl boldly "discovered" a bird from the torn pieces. This unintentional creation leads to awareness and exploration. Anything that does not achieve the desired result can be used as other means of expression. The piece that gets wet unintentionally can be modified to create other effect; the piece that is glued improperly can be treated as a kind of lively style; and the piece that is split into layers can be used to present different textures. In our creative team, we have artists with decades of experience, professional artists focusing on paper crafts, young paper collage lovers, and school kids with no "art literacy." Although we are all different, we share in the same vision: encourage discovery and strengthen self-confidence. Growing in this environment can stimulate new "discoveries," which promotes our techniques and art literacy.

Even though all styles, color combinations, and creativities can generate

Sky and Land
Paper: embossed paper, printing paper, and cardstock
Dimensions: 45 × 30 cm
In this collage, the sky and clouds are created with the splitting technique, whereas the land is constructed with the overlapping technique. The interaction between yin and yang as well as the correlation of virtuality and reality are deliberately set up on a flat piece of paper which is similar to an art print.

knowledge and theories, emotional expression is the most important in art creation. In order to have your own art style, every step requires practice. For beginners, getting experience through practices is way more important than learning the theories. This book helps you implement different elements through various lessons and artworks, collecting inspirations through imitative learning.

When you learn paper collage through imitation and shape your perception through our lessons, no need to tightly follow the "standards." Allowing differences will give you more space to discover the unexpected changes. Changes and differences are the hidden components for creativity. Learning from our lessons will give you more experience. When the time comes, you will have the drive to create independently. This is a positive sign. Feel free to find topics around you for creation. We suggest that in the beginning stage of independent creation, try to set up some simple targets such as style or color scheme. This process may not be as smooth as you wish but do not give up. It will help you gain deeper knowledge after imitating more artworks.

From beginning to end, we do believe paper collage is a very diverse and interesting art like a new game. There are more to be discovered and developed through different paper materials and themes. Learning paper collage can promote a collage lover to an artist. Let's begin with imitative learning.

CHAPTER TWO
Getting Ready

A fter learning the three main characteristics of paper collage and grasping the key points of imitative learning, you may have an itch for a try. With the theories in hand, are you still wondering out how to start? No problem! We will introduce paper collage materials, tools, and basic techniques in this chapter.

1. Materials

Paper is the main and only material in paper collage production process. Since paper collage has an irreproducible and flexible nature, selecting paper has a great deal of flexibility, allowing room for mistakes. When preparing the lessons for this book, we often arbitrarily selected from a large amount of different paper types. If the paper type was not available, we would substitute with another type that may come out with a surprise.

Different types of paper have different characteristics; different characteristics after different collage processing will deliver different effects. These effects should not be criticized as long as they bring forth an outstanding visual impact and reflect the artistic concept and expression. Any type, weight, or pattern of paper is an option. Here, we have neither an immutable color combination formula nor monotonous selection regulation. When you work on the lessons in chapters 3 and 4, no need to seek for the exact paper type. Use whatever you

Facing page
Chasing after Waves
Paper: embossed paper, printing paper, and sketch paper
Dimensions: 39 × 54 cm
With the use of colors in high density, this collage is created like an oil painting. The arrangement and layering of different colors well display the breaking waves. In the middle of the ocean, there is a sailboat chasing the waves. The red pieces not only emphasize the sailboat but also elevate the sense of danger.

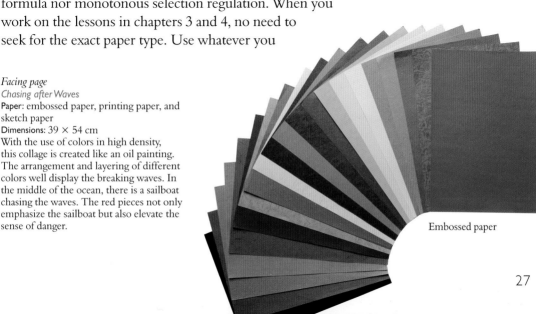

Embossed paper

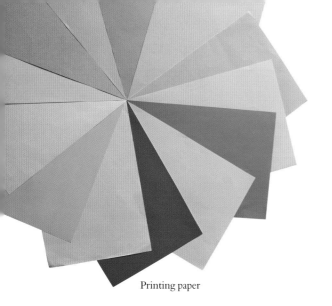

Printing paper

Card stock

have as long as you can construct an aesthetic paper collage with your own style.

For your reference, below is a list of paper that are commonly used in our lessons:

Embossed paper is produced by embossing machine, stamping patterns on the surface of paper. Its surface is a bit rough but with textures that have a strong presentation quality. There are a lot of different patterns such as twill, pebble, wave, cloud, basket weave, etc. Embossed paper is the most common material in this book.

Printing paper can be used for origami (paper folding) besides printing. It has a wide range of colors with a smooth surface. Its easy-to-tear characteristic is very suitable for modeling different styles.

Cardstock is thicker than writing paper but thinner than paperboard. The grammage is on the higher side. It has a smooth surface, high color purity and durability but less stretchability.

Translucent tracing paper is made by immersing the paper in sulfuric acid. It has a high quality, durability, and transparency. It can stand under heat and light with a non-deformed and non-aging nature. Artists like to use the translucent feature of tracing paper to illustrate the blur and crystal effects.

Sketch paper is usually white and thick, having rough texture and high density. Its fiber texture is commonly used to present an object's special feature. In this book, the white background of the paper collage is usually specified as sketch paper.

Poster paper with a smooth finish, is commonly used for printing magazines and posters. We can make use of the graphics, wordings, patterns, and colors of the printed matters to create and present our style and theme.

Tissue paper is an everyday item with a light, thin, soft, flexible, and stretchable nature. Different paper collage method generates different

Sketch paper

Poster paper

Tracing paper

Tissue paper

result. Crumpling or tearing can create a very special effect to present a particular feature.

2. Tools

Almost no tools are required for paper collage making. If there is one, it must be a simple one. The more complicated the tool is, the less flexible the paper collage will be generated. This will limit our creativity.

Our hands are the most important "tools" for paper collage making. All collage objects are required to be torn in pieces with our hands. Whether it is a light, heavy, slow, and rapid tearing, it directly affects the outcome. Our hands are the soul of paper collage art. They may be a bit stiff in the beginning and do not correspond to our expectation. Don't give up. Practice makes perfect.

Glue can secure the torn pieces on the background. Glue stick is the most popular adhesive tool since it has the least negative effect on paper collage making. Excessive glue will affect the neatness, aesthetic, and even the paper itself. That's why we have to avoid this kind of mistake.

Pencil and **eraser** are used to sketch the images. When we construct a complicated paper collage, we can use pencil to draw out the images and then tear, so that the components are more controllable and neat.

Knife is a supplementary tool. Since our hands cannot accurately tear small pieces, we can make use of a knife to cut extra small pieces.

From left to right: glue, pencil, eraser and knife.

3. Basic Techniques

The techniques of paper collage making are not complicated. They are mainly operated by our hands with different motions. The physical agility of our hands has a direct influence on the result. We hope we can continue to practice so that our hands are more flexible. Here, we have collected the techniques of paper collage making for your reference.

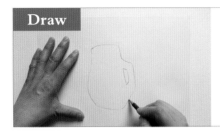

Draw

When we try to tear a complicated piece, especially for beginners, we can first draw the outline of the components on the paper as an aid.

Fold

When we need a straight edge, we can first fold the paper and then tear along the fold. This can produce a neat edge.

Tear

Use your thumbs and index fingers to hold and pull apart a piece of paper until the cross section is shown. The torn edge is usually a bit rough.

Split

Split is to separate the surface of a paper to expose the fiber texture. Splitting and tearing usually work together to reveal the fiber at the torn edge to obtain an artistic effect.

Cut

When getting into details, our bare hands may not be accurate enough. We can use a knife to cut but do not over use it; otherwise the paper collage will lose its identity.

Crumple

Place a piece of paper on your palm; then make a fist to crumple it. A number of folds will be naturally formed, which can be a base of a component.

Pinch

Use your thumb and index finger to pinch a line on a piece of paper to make a flat surface three-dimensional. It commonly works with crumpling.

Overlap

Placing a piece of paper on top of another piece to produce an overlapping visual effect, which enhances the layering and three-dimensional effects.

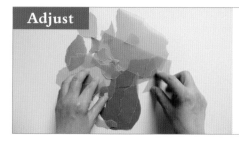

Adjust

After placing a piece of paper or assembling, we need to adjust the layout to achieve the designated visual effect. All paper collage works require continuous adjustments to accomplish a better result.

Glue

After adjustment, use glue stick to adhere the pieces to the background or other pieces. When gluing, try to use as less glue as possible to attain the neatness.

There is no absolute regulation. When you create your paper collage, wisely use your wisdom and hands to innovate or simplify techniques that are suitable for you in order to accomplish a brilliant artwork. Same as what we have emphasized before, paper collage is not immutable. Continuous revolution can make your work sparkle!

CHAPTER THREE
Introductory Lessons

I n this chapter, we will elaborate on the basic key points, methods, styles and characteristics of paper collage through a collection of projects, starting from the fundamental and simplest ones so that we can learn this art step by step.

Here, we would like to highlight that a lot of the projects were created 20 years ago. They are: *Flowers in a Vase (Abstract Expressionism)*, *Flowers in a Vase (Watercolor Style)*, *Chrysanthemums*, *Daffodils*, *Morning Glory* and *The Warm Sun*. To tie in with the lessons, we have reproduced some of the artworks. Compare the first image with the last one in the lessons, you will find that some dissimilarities between the two. The flexibility and irreproducible nature of paper collage is very pronounced. To make the instructions clearer, our lessons are standardized, but you do not have to follow every single step during the process. You can tear out a piece and glue, tear out a bunch then arrange, or tear out all components then assemble and set on the background. Feel free to boldly create according to your preferences and habits to fully unleash your initiative to create a piece of paper collage art in your own style.

Now let's start the journey of paper collage!

The Cranes
Paper: embossed paper, crepe paper, cardstock, and tissue
Dimensions: 54 × 39 cm
This collage is composed by crumpling the bluish and greenish paper to create the green vegetation and blue sea. The creases make the background scene more three-dimensional. Nevertheless, the clouds in the sky are formed by layers of soft tissue. The main theme—cranes—is constructed by overlapping the paper pieces with detailed configuration of the wings, delivering a celestial scene.

1. Two Basic Styles

In any form of art, the most important is to establish the concept and present the object. For drawing, we use different types of pens and brushes to picture on a piece of paper or other media. For sculpting, we use knives to shape on a piece of wood or other materials. For paper collage, we first need to figure out the shape of the object. How do we utilize the torn pieces of different sizes, shape and outlines? Here, we have summarized into two methods:

Component tearing method. This is to directly tear the paper according to the shape of the object. The advantage of this method is to create a complete and clear style. The outlines are smoother.

Scrap assembling method. First is to tear the paper into different forms and then assemble the fragments to form the shape of the object. The advantage of this method is to provide more freedom and flexibility for assembling. The overlapping of the scraps can also help elevate the three-dimensional effect.

We can select one of these two basic techniques according to the actual condition in order to fully express our concept. Usually, we combine both techniques to enhance the diversity and layering effect. In the following lessons, we will use both techniques to fabricate the same theme so that we can experience the different effects during the production.

Swirling Clouds
Paper: embossed paper, cardstock, and printing paper
Dimensions: 25 × 25 cm
Putting aside the bright colors, this collage is based on cold colors and created in a casual style to present the swirling clouds in the sky and scattered bushes on the earth.

The Giant Panda

The giant panda is a special species from China. It is known as the "living fossil" since it has been around for more than eight hundred years. Due to the scarcity, the giant panda is often offered as a diplomatic gift to other countries. The history of serving as an "ambassador" can be dated back to the period (624–705) when Empress Wu Zetian gave two giant pandas to Japan.

This piece of art applies the method of component tearing: using the black and white glossy paper, directly tear out the head, body, limbs and facial features of the giant panda, and place them on a landscape scene taking from a magazine as the background. The giant panda, lying on the lawn and licking its arm, looks very lively, adorable and charmingly naive. You can choose your own background, which can be grassland, bamboo grove, or any other natural environment to create different effects.

Paper: white, lake blue and black cardstock.
Background: landscape image from magazine
(20 × 20 cm).

1 Split the white cardstock into two from the edge. If the cardstock cannot be split from the middle, you can choose other types of paper. Paper collage can be very creative and unrestrained that allows you to use different types of paper material.

2 As shown, the top part is the paper surface whereas the bottom part is the fiber from the torn area. We can use the rough texture to present the furry giant panda.

3 Tear an egg shape from the rough white cardstock to form the body of the giant panda.

4 Similar to step 3, tear out the head of the giant panda.

5 Tear the 2 forelimbs and 1 hind limb of the giant panda from the black cardstock. The 2 forelimbs are sturdier. Do not tear in a neat and clear manner. Simply leave the fiber texture to deliver the furry effect.

6 Tear the semicircular ears and oval shaped eyes and nose from the black cardstock.

7 Tear 3 strips from the lake blue cardstock as the shadows.

8 Choose a landscape image from a magazine and cut it to the proper size.

9 Place the body of the giant panda in the middle of the landscape image.

10 Put the left forelimb onto the lower right of the body. Note that the body overlaps the left forelimb.

11 Place the right forelimb onto the middle of the body. Note that the right forelimb overlaps the body.

12 Add the hind limb on top of the left side of the body.

13 Place the head onto the lower right of the body and between the 2 forelimbs. Attach the pair of the ears on top of the head.

14 Add the eyes and nose.

15 Place the lake blue shadows below the body. Adjust and secure the overall layout.

The Giant Panda Head

We have made a creeping giant panda in the previous lesson using the component tearing method. In this lesson, we will introduce how to deliver the same theme by applying the scrap assembling method.

This giant panda is a collection of black and white cardstock of different sizes and shapes. It has a stronger three-dimensional and furry effect.

Paper: white and black cardstock.
Background: dark green embossed paper (21 × 30 cm).

1 Split the white cardstock into two from the edge. Use the exposed fiber from the torn area to present the furry giant panda.

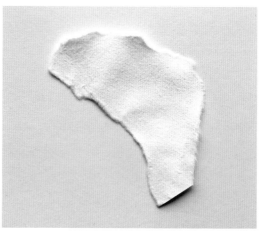

2 Tear out a large crescent from the white cardstock as the base of the giant panda head.

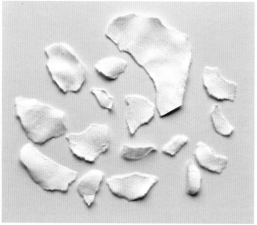

3 Tear a number of small white pieces in different sizes and shapes.

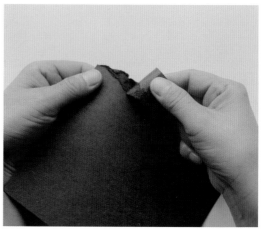

4 Tear and split the black cardstock at the same time to create the irregular edge so that the rough texture can present the furry effect.

5 Follow step 5 to produce the ears, eyes, and nose.

6 Place the white crescent onto the right center of the background. This is the top part of the giant panda head.

7 Add the small white pieces to outline the lower part of the head.

8 Add more white pieces around the brow ridge, cheekbones, and nasal bone to promote the three-dimensional effect on the face.

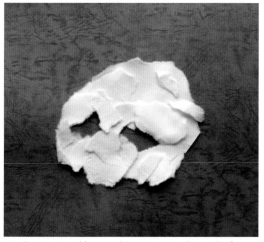

9 Continue to add more white pieces to enhance the furry effect.

10 Place the ears above the head.

11 Place the nose onto the lower part of the head.

12 Lastly, add the eyes. Adjust and secure the overall collage.

2. Capturing Special Features

After learning how to establish the overall style of an art subject, we will learn how to capture the special features to boost the style in this session.

Everything in the world has a different form and characteristics. There are two ways to differentiate and capture the features: directly depict the features of the subject and indirectly depict the features of the subject through the surrounding objects.

The first method is to directly target on the unique feature of the subject; for example, the fork-tail of a swallow, the fluttering of a willow tree, and the blue raging waves of the sea. Furthermore, we can distinguish the features between a hen and chicken, a male and female bird, and among different dog breeds.

The second method is to use the movement of the surrounding objects to present the features of the invisible subject; for example, use the swirling petals to present the feature of wind, and use the wandering fishes and the flow of bubbles to present the feature of underwater.

We need the notion of awareness to observe the surrounding objects and capture the main features of them. Interchanging the two methods can improve the presentation of your paper collage artworks.

Sunrise
Paper: embossed paper and printing paper
Dimensions: 25 × 25 cm
With the reference of impressionism, large amount of small paper pieces is used to simulate the brushstroke and lighting effect of impressionistic painting, depicting the scene of sunrise sparkling on the endless ocean, creating the interaction between the light and shadow.

Penguins

Penguins are the oldest natatores and largest flightless birds. They are mainly found in the southern hemisphere, especially in the Antarctic regions. People love them for their naive appearance and vigorous swimming style.

Before we start, let's summarize the distinctive features of the penguins. The black head, back, and wings with the white belly are their color features; the chubby body, little head, and tapered wings are the appearance features; the standing gesture and flippers are the figure features; the blue sky, glaciers, and icebergs are the habitation features. The first three features are their subjective features while the last one is the feature of their surroundings. Capturing these features can transform the torn pieces to a natural scene of Antarctic regions.

Paper: white glossy cardstock; navy blue and dark gray cardstock; dark red and sky blue embossed paper; off-white and gray printing paper.
Background: lake blue printing paper (20 × 20 cm).

1 Tear 2 irregular trapezoids from the sky blue embossed paper.

2 Using the lake blue printing paper as the background, place the sky blue pieces in the middle as the icebergs.

3 Tear 2 irregular pieces from the white printing paper as the clouds or glaciers.

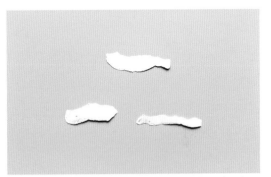

4 Tear 3 cloudlike pieces from the white glossy cardstock as the waves or clouds.

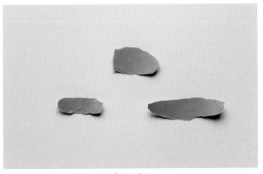

5 Tear 3 irregular pieces from the gray printing paper.

6 Place the large piece of glacier below the icebergs.

7 Add the 3 gray pieces onto the glacier as the shadows. Note the sense of scattering.

8 Place the 2 white cloudlike pieces below the glacier as the waves.

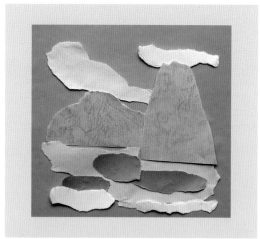

9 Add 2 white clouds above the icebergs.

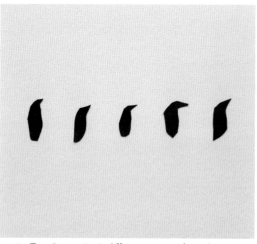

10 Tear 5 penguins in different gestures from the navy blue cardstock.

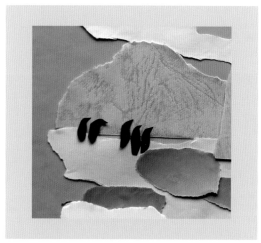

11 Place them above the glacier of the far side in perspective view.

12 Tear the chubby body with the two short feet of the penguin in the middle from the white glossy cardstock.

13 Tear the body of the other penguin from the white glossy paper and tear the body of the small penguin from the off-white printing paper. We use different colors for the bodies to distinguish penguins in different ages.

14 Tear the head and wings of the small penguin from the dark gray cardstock.

15 Use the same method to tear the heads and wings of the 2 big penguins from the navy blue cardstock.

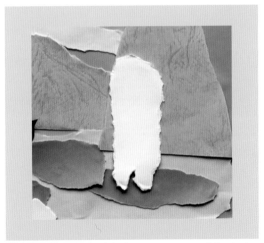

16 Place the body of the big penguin on top of the shadow in the front.

17 Add the head and wings onto the body.

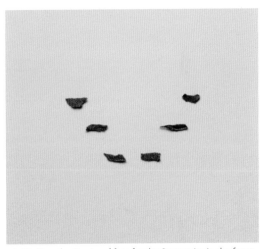

18 Tear the 3 pairs of feet for the 3 penguins in the front from the dark red embossed paper.

19 Add a pair of dark red feet below the body of the big penguin.

20 Repeat the above step for the 2 penguins next to it. Note the interaction between the middle big penguin and the small one; adjust and set the overall layout.

Goldfish

The goldfish is a domesticated version of the carp family. Chinese began to breed different varieties long time ago. The goldfishes all around the world nowadays are directly or indirectly from the Chinese establishment. They are very popular due to the diverse varieties and colors. In Chinese New Year, people like to buy a pair of goldfishes as a symbol of bringing wealth and wishing for surplus.

This piece of artwork captures the features of goldfish—the translucent eyes and fins. Tracing paper is used to present these features as well as the water, making the relaxed wandering fish true to life.

Paper: emerald, ultramarine and violet embossed paper; white crepe paper; lake blue, orange-red, sky blue and navy blue printing paper; pink and yellow tracing paper.

Background: sky blue printing paper (30 × 21 cm).

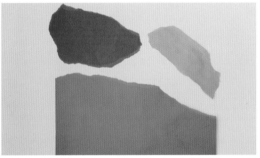

1 Tear a few irregular pieces from the ultramarine and emerald embossed paper as well as the lake blue printing paper as shown. This is the background elements of the pond.

2 Place the emerald element on the sky blue background paper. Note that the 3 sides of the emerald element align with the background paper.

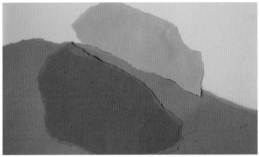

3 Place the ultramarine and lake blue elements in the middle.

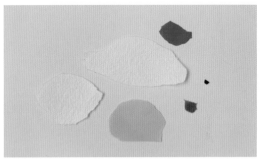

4 Tear different parts of the goldfish from papers. Do not restrict the color usage relative to the body parts. Feel free to play around with it.

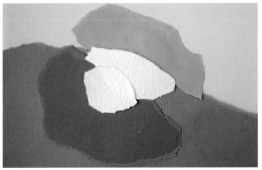

5 Place the goldfish body using the white crepe paper in the center.

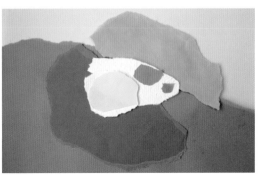

6 Add the eye and patterns of the goldfish.

7 Tear a number of pieces in different sizes and shapes from the pink tracing paper as the fins.

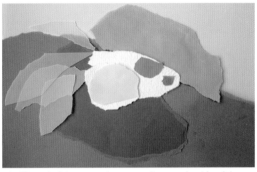

8 Place the biggest tracing paper piece on the side of the body as the caudal fin.

9 Continue to add the smaller tracing paper pieces around the caudal fin.

10 Arrange the anal fin above the belly.

11 Add the pectoral, pelvic and dorsal fins. Stacking the tracing paper pieces can enhance the layering and three-dimensional effects.

12 Use the pink and yellow tracing paper to tear out the pieces as shown.

13 Place the big pink tracing paper piece on the lower right to present the water.

14 Add the smaller pink and yellow tracing paper pieces around as the bubbles.

15 Tear a number of small irregular pieces from the ultramarine and emerald embossed paper.

16 Scatter them around as the water plants in the pond. Adjust and set the overall layout.

Flowers and Birds Bathing in the Moonlight

In Chinese literature, "blooming flowers under full moon" and "magpie on plum blossoms" are auspicious idioms about perfect life. This piece of art combines these two idioms, illustrating a harmonized nature scene of blooming flowers, shining moon, lovely birds, and serene night.

This paper collage does not reflect the original colors of the birds. Instead, it captures their features such as the details of the tails, sharpness of the beaks, and chubbiness of the bellies, clearly expressing the pure and deep artistic concept. It does not follow the traditional approach but use the green tracing paper as the main material. The transparent tracing paper is the best mean to illustrate the silhouette of the flowers and birds against the moonlight. The black background enhances the mysterious effect.

What you have to pay attention to is the use of glue. Using less glue as much as possible, otherwise, it will affect the translucency of tracing paper and the collage may lose the crystal effect.

Paper: green tracing and white cardstock.
Background: black cardstock (30 × 20 cm).

1 Tear 2 identical round pieces from the green tracing paper and white cardstock. Then tear another round piece that is a bit bigger from the green tracing paper.

2 Tear various parts of the bird on the left from the green tracing paper. Be sure to bring out the side profile.

3 Tear a few long strips from the green tracing paper as the branches. One of them is a long forked branch.

4 Place the small green round piece on the black background.

5 Add the white round piece above the green around piece, having the lower right edge of the green piece exposed.

6 Place the bigger green round piece on top of the white piece. A hazy moon is formed.

7 Place the body of the bird on the left side of the moon.

8 Add the long forked branch below the feet. A resting bird on the tree begins to form.

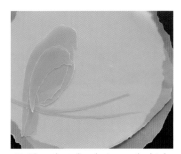

9 Place the tail and wing on the bird.

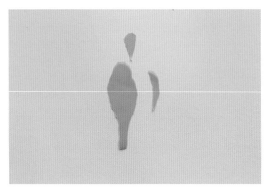

10 Tear various parts of the bird on the right from the green tracing paper. Note that this bird is facing to the front.

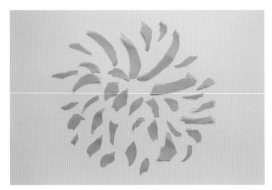

11 Tear a number of irregular pieces from the green tracing paper as the flowers and leaves.

12 Place the plume and beak from step 2 on the head.

13 Place the bird from step 10 on the right side of the branch. It is nestling up against the other bird.

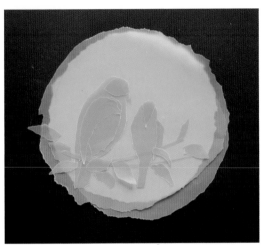

14 Place the flowers and leaves on the forked branch.

15 Place the branches on the lower right of the forked branch. Add some flowers and leaves for enhancement.

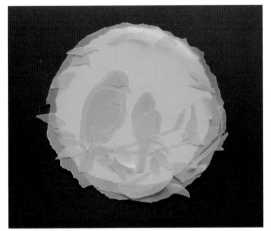

16 Place more flowers, leaves, and branches around the perimeter of the moon. Be sure to scatter them to create a beautiful scene of fallen petals.

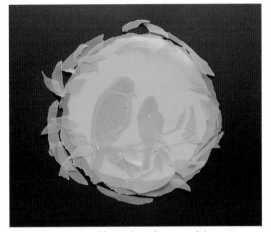

17 Continue to add more branches around the perimeter of the moon with flowers and leaves to enhance the layering effect. Adjust and set the overall layout.

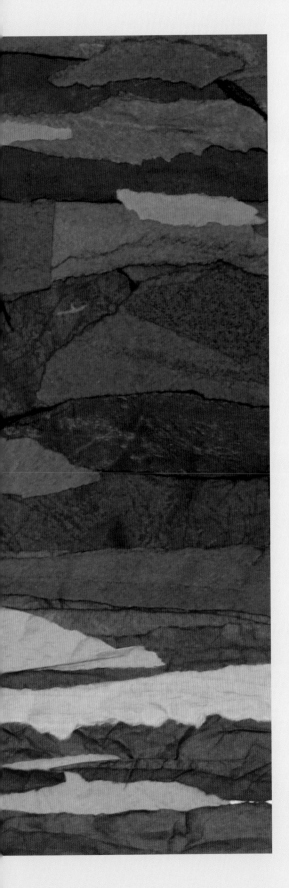

3. Deformation and Exaggeration

Deformation and exaggeration are the common techniques of paper collage. Deformation is to change the form of the subject whereas exaggeration is to magnify the features or motions of the subjects to make the art more lifelike and eye-catching. These two methods are commonly used together.

No leaves are identical. An artist cannot reproduce two identical paper collage works. Paper collage is flexible and features freehand styles. After learning how to capture the special features, beginners can boldly transform with appropriate exaggeration to create a paper collage with personal and unique style.

As we have emphasized before, you do not have to blindly follow every single step as listed on the lessons. Use your creativity and imagination, which may bring you an unexpected reward.

The Moon
Paper: embossed paper and printing paper
Dimensions: 25 × 25 cm
This paper collage is divided into 2 portions: the upper part is the sky in cold tone whereas the lower half is the land in warm tone. The crumpling technique produces lots of creases to form the uneven land. Meanwhile, the half-moon hiding in the clouds points out the theme of this art.

The Winding Path to the Secluded Place

The winding path leads to the secluded place,
The Buddhist temple is secreted in the blossoming flowers.

This is extracted from a famous poem by Chang Jian (708–*unknown*), a poet of the Tang dynasty (618–907). He diverts his affections on the nature and leaves behind the worldly customs, yearning for the seclusion and Zen serenity.

This collage is derived from the concept of the above poem, illustrating a winding path to the woods. The path gradually disappears as it meets the sky, connoting the idea of Zen, which make the viewers fall into reveries. Through the transformation and exaggeration of woods and path, this piece of art fully demonstrates the carefree and liberal style.

Paper: sky blue and lake blue printing paper; white cardstock; light ocher, dark gray, black, grass green, dark green, emerald, navy blue and ultramarine embossed paper.
Background: white cardstock (25 × 30 cm).
Tool: knife.

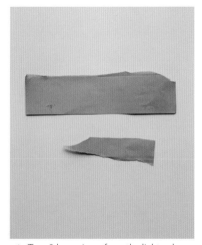

1 Tear 2 long pieces from the light ocher embossed paper.

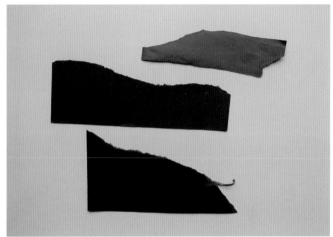

2 Tear 3 pieces as shown from the navy blue and ultramarine embossed paper.

3 Tear 2 small pieces from the sky blue and lake blue printing paper.

4 Tear a few pieces as shown on the picture from the black embossed paper.

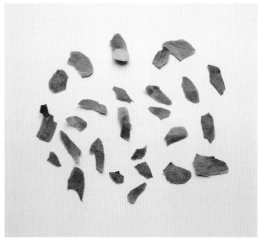

5 Tear a number of small irregular pieces from the dark gray embossed paper as stones on the winding path.

6 Tear a few small pieces from the light ocher embossed paper.

7 Tear 2 pieces as shown from the grass green and dark green embossed paper.

8 Tear 2 pieces as shown from the grass green and emerald embossed paper.

9 Tear several long pieces from the grass green, dark green and emerald embossed paper.

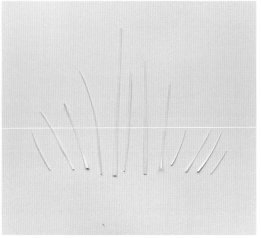

10 Use a knife to cut several long and thin branches and trunks from the white cardstock.

11 Place the 2 light ocher pieces on the top part of the background, overlapping one another as the sky.

12 Place the 3 pieces from step 2 in the center of the background, overlapping each other as the ground in the middle of the collage.

13 Place the sky blue piece on the sky as the cloud and the lake blue piece on where the sky meets the ground as part of the mountain from afar.

14 Place the black pieces at the bottom of the collage as the ground in front. Put one of them on the lake blue piece to complete the distant mountain scene.

15 Place the dark gray stones on the black ground at the lower part of the collage, forming a C shape.

16 Continue to add more dark gray stones to complete the winding path.

17 Scatter the light ocher pieces from step 6 on the winding path, using different color tones to depict the uneven and muddy path.

18 Place the green pieces from step 7 on the left side of the collage as the trees.

19 Place the pieces from step 8 on the right side of the collage, overlapping each other as the trees.

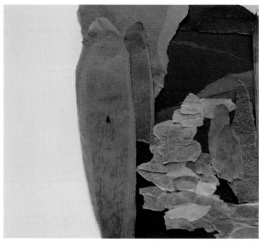

20 Place the long pieces from setp 9 on the left side of the collage.

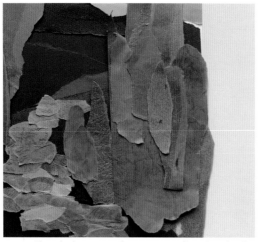

21 Place the long pieces from setp 9 on the right side of the collage to form a luxuriant feel.

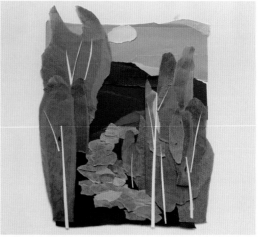

22 Place the white trunks on the trees. Then add the branches accordingly. Adjust and set the overall layout.

Mother and Son

Leopards have spots on their bodies. Some are like Chinese coins and thus they are called "golden coin leopards" in China. "Viewing a leopard through a bamboo allows you to see the pattern" is a Chinese idiom meaning observing a small part of an object allows us to guess the overall picture. In the philosophical point of view, we can get the generality when knowing the particularity. This idiom can fully interpret this lesson.

This collage successfully captures the spots as the special feature so that the main subject—leopards—is clearly acknowledged. At the same time, the leopards are properly exaggerated and boldly transformed, personifying a ferocious leopard to a cute cartoon character. With the little leopard playing around, a picture of mother and son is created.

Paper: white, black, tangerine and orange-red cardstock; sky blue, light brown, violet, yellow and dark brown embossed paper.
Background: white cardstock (20 × 30 cm).
Tool: scissors.

1 Tear a piece as shown from the sky blue embossed paper.

2 Add the sky blue piece onto the top right of the white background as the cave at the back.

3 Tear a piece as shown from the violet embossed paper.

4 Place the violet piece on the bottom of the white background as the shadow of the cave.

5 Tear an oval piece from the tangerine cardstock as the body of the leopard mother.

6 Tear 2 forelimbs and 1 hind limb of the mother from the tangerine cardstock.

7 Tear a pair of ears, head, neck and tail of the mother from the tangerine cardstock.

8 Tear its face and belly from the white cardstock. Then tear its eyes, nose and mouth from the black cardstock.

9 Cut its whiskers from the dark brown embossed paper.

10 Assemble its ear, head and neck on the cave.

11 Arrange its body and belly below the neck.

12 Add the 2 forelimbs. Note that one limb is behind the body and the other is above the belly.

13 Place the hind limb and tail on the lower right of the body.

14 Add the face, eyes, nose, mouth and whiskers onto the head.

15 Use the same method to tear the body parts of the little leopard.

16 Assemble the little leopard nestling against its mother's forelimb.

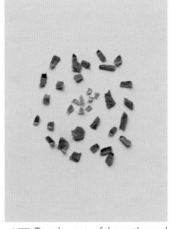

17 Tear the spots of the mother and son from the yellow and light brown embossed paper.

18 Lastly, place the spots on the bodies. Adjust and set the overall layout.

4. Generalization and Simplification

Step by step, we have learned from the previous three sections the basic skills and key points of how to tear out a subject. We believe you have seized how to produce various styles. From certain points of view, these three methods still concentrate on the figurative presentation; but in order to use the simplest and most appropriate style to express the various features of different subjects we need to learn how to generalize the objects. This is the most difficult part of paper collage making.

Due to the characteristics of paper and limitation of paper tearing, the products that are made by our hands are not as smooth, refined, and complicated as those that are cut from the scissors. The outlines and styles of paper tearing products are usually rough, general, and simple. The skills of generalization and simplification do not only lower the difficulties of paper collage making but also extend the flexibility and imagination during the process of creating as well as testing the artist's ability and overall art sense. We will use a few projects to demonstrate the artistic concept of returning to original nature which is not equal to laziness and tricks.

The Village
Paper: embossed paper, cardstock, and printing paper
Dimensions: 20 × 20 cm
Getting the idea from Wassily Kandinsky, an influential Russian painter and founder of abstract art, this collage collects the bright colors and abstract forms to compose a village scene in oil painting style.

The Fox Borrowing the Awe of the Tiger

The idiom "the fox borrowing the awe of the tiger" is extracted from one of the ancient Chinese fables. One day, a tiger caught a fox as his lunch. The fox declared to the tiger that he was the king of beasts and it was against Heaven's will to kill him. Seeing that the tiger might be dubious, the fox asked the tiger to follow him to meet the beasts. When the beasts saw them, they all ran away. This made the tiger believe in what the fox had said without realizing the fact that the beasts were actually afraid of him walking behind the fox. This idiom is often used to analogize to those who rely on others' power to oppress other people.

This art piece firmly grasps the main features of the subjects: the pattern of the tiger and the tail of the fox. Besides catching the features, it also generalizes and simplifies the trees, underbrush, fox and tiger without ignoring the details to naturally deliver the fable.

Paper: olive green, emerald, blackish green and ocher embossed paper; tangerine, orange-red, black and white cardstock; lake blue and pastel green printing paper.
Background: navy blue embossed paper (20 × 30 cm).

1 Tear a number of strips in different lengths from the ocher embossed paper.

2 Tear several strips from the emerald embossed paper.

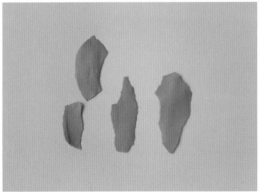

3 Tear a few irregular pieces from the lake blue printing paper.

4 Tear a number of irregular pieces from the olive green embossed paper.

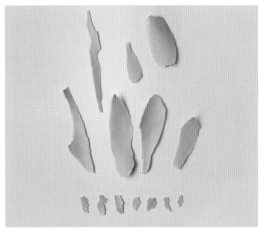

5 Tear a number of pieces in different sized from the pastel green printing paper. The larger ones are leaves whereas the smaller ones are used as grass or lawn.

6 Tear different parts of the tiger from the orange-red, white, and black cardstock as well as the ocher embossed paper.

7 Assemble the tiger parts.

8 Tear the body of the fox from the tangerine cardstock. Note the feature of the fox's tail and arrogant gesture when it pretends to be the king of beasts, as well as the relative body size.

9 Use the blackish green, ocher, and emerald embossed paper to tear the pieces as shown on the diagram as the background scene. They can be trees, underbrush, rocks.

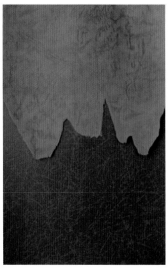

10 Place the blackish green piece on the top part of the navy blue background as the forest. Note that the top and side edges align with the background.

11 Place the ocher and emerald pieces on the bottom as the underbrush and bushes.

12 Add 4 thicker and longer ocher strips as the trunks. The closer the view is, the thicker the trunk to be.

13 Continue to add the thinner ocher trunks.

14 Place the shorter ocher strips on the trunks as the branches. Note that the branches are in different angles.

15 Add the emerald strips among the ocher trunks. They are also the trunks.

16 Place the olive green pieces on the top part of the background as the leaves.

17 Continue to add the lake blue pieces on top. Place some olive green pieces below as the underbrush.

18 Place the pastel green leaves on top of the other leaves to enhance the layering effect. Add the pastel green grass on the underbrush to enrich the scene.

19 Place the tiger onto the bottom of the picture. Place the fox in front of the tiger. Adjust and set the overall layout.

Relaxing Sparrows

Sparrows resting on the high-voltage cables is a very common picture. This piece of art is derived from a daily scene, bringing forth the colors and features of the blue sky, white clouds, green trees, and sparrows by means of generalization and simplification.

In this collage, the image of the high-voltage cable is not presented in the mainstream format such as placing a black line on top. Instead, the sky blue paper is separated into two with the black paper at the back. This is like using the cable to tear the sky forming a gap in between, which demonstrates the ultimate level of generalization and simplification.

Paper: black, ocher and white cardstock; navy blue, lake blue, sky blue, emerald and blackish green embossed paper.
Background: sky blue embossed paper (21 × 30 cm).

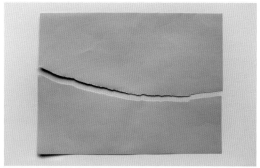

1 Separate the sky blue embossed paper into half. The tear is curved, setting for the high-voltage cable.

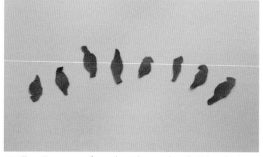

2 Tear a rectangle from the black cardstock. The width is to be the same as the sky blue embossed paper.

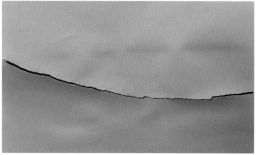

3 Place the black rectangle beneath the sky blue background so that the black cardstock is naturally shown as the high-voltage cable.

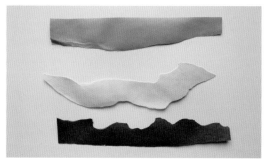

4 Tear a few irregular pieces from the lake blue, sky blue, and navy blue embossed paper as the scene at the back.

5 Tear 1 big and 2 small clouds from the white cardstock. Be sure to tear and split at the same time to present the fluffiness of the clouds through the rough texture.

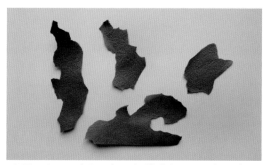

6 Tear 4 serrated pieces from the blackish green embossed paper as the trees. This is a high level of generalization and simplification of tree crowns and trunks.

7 Same as step 6, tear a few smaller emerald and lake blue embossed paper as the bushes.

8 Tear 8 sparrows from the ocher cardstock. Take a look at them carefully. Their heads, tails, and bodies are in different gestures.

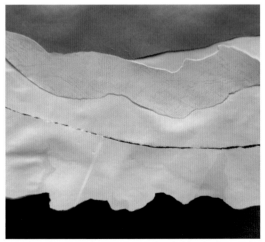

9 Place the pieces from step 4 on the sky blue background, arranged from light to dark as the sky and bushes.

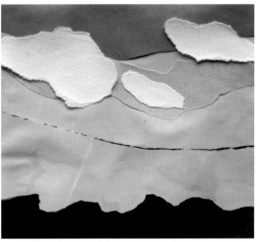

10 Place the 3 clouds from step 5 on the sky.

11 Place the 4 blackish green trees from step 6 on the lower part of the picture.

12 Add the emerald and lake blue bushes from step 7 onto the lower part of the picture.

13 Place 3 sparrows as a group on the right side of the cable. Note that they are in different elevations.

14 Place the other 3 groups of sparrows. Note the interaction among them. Adjust and set the overall layout.

Standing by a Tree Stump Waiting for a Hare

The idiom "standing by a tree stump waiting for a hare" is written by Han Fei (280–233 BC), a Chinese influential political and Legalism philosopher of the Warring States period(475–221 BC). In his classical writings *Han Feizi*, there is a story talking about a farmer who saw a hare run into a tree accidentally and died. He decided not to work hard anymore and waited by the tree stump, hoping that another hare would be killed by the trump. However, he wasted the field and got teased by his neighbors. This story tells us that it is impossible to reap without sowing. The only way is to work hard to get what we want.

   This piece of artwork captures the main features of the subjects as well as generalizing the simplifying of the hare and farmer, fully expressing the laziness of the farmer and the death of the hare. The leaves here are not in the regular oval shape. Instead, they are presented in two colors and form of layering to enhance the luxuriance.

Paper: navy blue, violet, emerald and black embossed paper; tangerine, lemon, sky blue, lake blue and white printing paper.
Background: pink cardstock (30 × 21 cm).

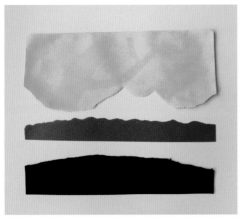

1 Tear large pieces from the lemon printing paper, emerald and black embossed paper as the tree crown, underbrush, and soil respectively.

2 Add the lemon tree crown and emerald underbrush onto the pink background. Place the black soil on the emerald underbrush. Be sure to leave the emerald edge so that it looks like a farmland from afar.

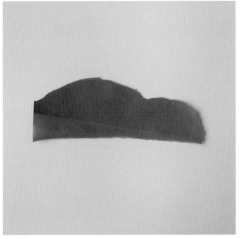

3 Tear a piece as shown from the violet embossed paper.

4 Place it onto the lower left of the picture as the bushes.

5 Tear a piece as shown from the navy blue embossed paper as the tree trunk and branches.

6 Place the navy blue trunk and branches on the left of the collage.

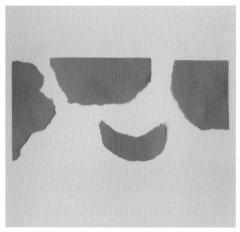

7 Tear several irregular pieces as shown from the tangerine printing paper.

8 Place the tangerine leaves on the lemon crown. Note that some of the leaves are above and some are below the crown to create the sense of layering.

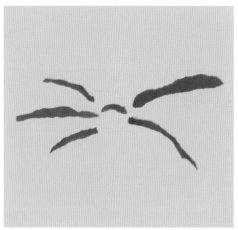

9 Tear a few thin strips from the emerald embossed paper.

10 Place them on the black soil. This is also a generalization and simplification of the lawn to present the overgrown farmland on the near side.

11 Tear the farmer's hat, head, shoes, and body from papers of different colors. Note that the farmer is in a sitting position. Be sure the body and leg are related to the sitting gesture.

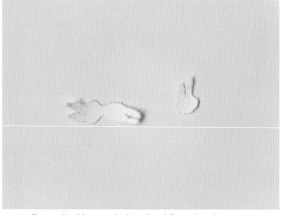

12 Tear a dead hare and a hare head from the white printing paper. Note the gesture of the dead hare.

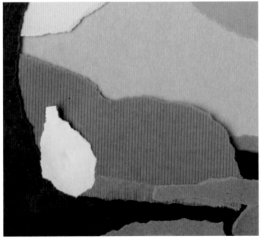

13 Add the sky blue body leaning against the trunk.

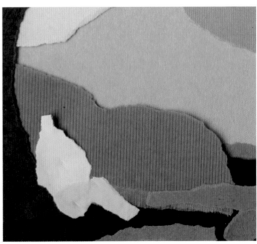

14 Place the lake blue leg below the body.

15 Add the farmer's head and hand.

16 Put the lemon hat on his head. We do not pay too much attention on the details. Instead, we polish the features to express an idle farmer using generalization and simplification.

17 Place the dead hare below the tree.

18 Place the hare head onto the far side. Adjust and set the overall layout.

Starry Sky

In this paper collage, the clear pond, green tree, starry sky, and little girl are all captured here to express a harmonized picture between humans and nature. The sky represents the unlimited universe whereas the girl symbolizes the littleness as a human comparing to the universe. The whole picture reflects the endless exploration of the unknown universe, configuring a lovely scene with bottomless artistic concept.

The main focus of this artwork is to engage the overall atmosphere by using the ultimate generalization to illustrate all the components. No matter whether it is the pond, tree or girl, all are simple and yet sophisticated. Every single component captures the features of what you can see at night, showing a natural and lively scene.

Paper: pink, pale yellow, yellow, red and black cardstock; light green, dark green and cobalt blue embossed paper.
Background: tangerine cardstock (20 × 20 cm).
Tool: scissors.

1 Cut the black cardstock to a square. Tear and split it to expose the rough texture.

2 Tear it as shown. Note the texture at the edge.

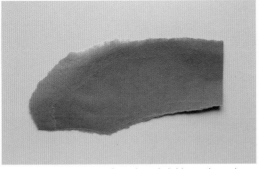

3 Tear a piece as shown from the cobalt blue embossed paper. Note the texture at the edges again.

4 Tear a tree from the dark green embossed paper. Note the outline of the edges.

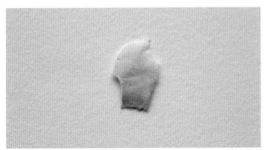

5 Tear out the girl's chiffon dress from the pink cardstock. Pay attention to the texture at the edges to emphasize the translucent effect. Be sure the shape of the dress matches the body shape of the girl.

6 Tear out the girl's hair from the black cardstock. Note that the girl's back is facing us, so the hair has to match the overall shape of her head.

7 Tear out the girl's hands and legs from the pale yellow cardstock.

8 Tear out a pair of shoes from the red cardstock.

9 Place the black piece on the tangerine background. Be sure to align the bottom and side edges with the background. This is the land. You can see that the textured edge looks like the landscape from afar.

10 Place the cobalt blue piece on the black land. The right edge aligns with the background. This is the pond.

11 Place the green tree on the left side of the pond.

12 Place the chiffon dress on the lower right of the pond.

13 Add the hair above the dress. Be sure to mimic the gesture of the girl with her head up counting the stars.

14 Add the hands and legs for the girl.

15 Put the shoes on for the girl.

16 Cut a few strips from the light green embossed paper. Then turn them horizontally, cut them into small pieces and scatter them on the collage as the twinkling stars.

17 Repeat step 16 on the pale yellow cardstock and scatter the small pieces on the collage as the stars.

18 Then work on the yellow cardstock and scatter the stars on the collage.

19 The light green, pale yellow, and yellow stars are scattered on the picture but they are messy.

20 Arrange the stars so that they look naturally covering the sky and pond. Adjust and set the overall layout.

The Street View

This paper collage is based on what you can see every day on streets of a metropolitan city using one-point perspective. The overlaying of the geometrical components turns the picture to be abstract and yet fully illustrates the clusters of highrises in a city. The overlapping of the rectangles and intersecting of the edges well portray the scene of row upon row of buildings. The translucency of the tracing paper artfully portrays the silhouette of the buildings afar and flashing billboards. Meanwhile, the pedestrians walking on the streets highlight the "street view" theme and build in more energy for the collage.

Paper: black and white cardstock; green, red, blue and yellow tracing paper.
Background: blue tracing paper (21 × 30 cm).
Tool: knife.

1 Cut 3 rectangles from the yellow and blue tracing paper as shown. These are the buildings. To make them neat and clean, you can use a knife.

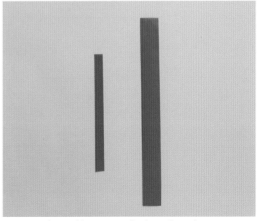

2 Cut 2 big trapezoids from the white cardstock.

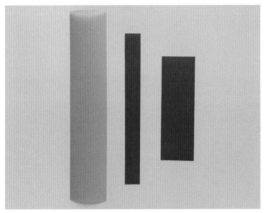

3 Cut 2 small rectangles from the blue tracing paper.

4 Cut 2 thin and long rectangles from the red tracing paper.

5 Cut 2 big rectangles from the green tracing paper.

6 Cut a big rectangle from the yellow tracing paper and chamfer one corner.

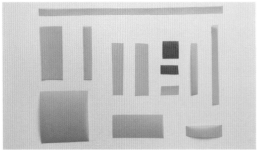

7 Cut a number of rectangles in different sizes from the red, green, and yellow tracing paper.

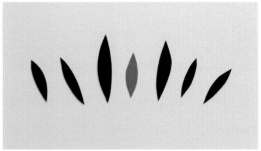

8 Cut several fusiforms from the black cardstock and red tracing paper as the abstract human figures.

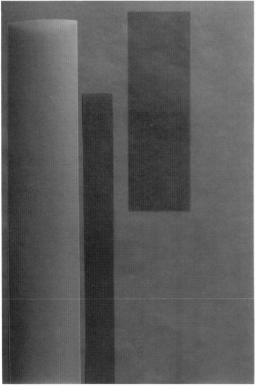

9 Place the 3 rectangles from step 1 on the blue tracing paper background. Note that the 2 blue rectangles can be placed on top or below the background, which will create different effects due to the translucency of tracing paper.

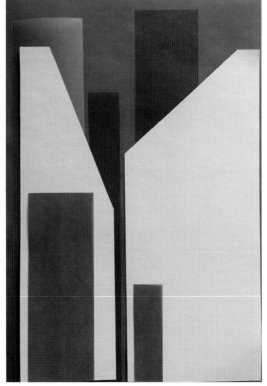

10 Place the 2 white trapezoids on two sides. Place the 2 blue rectangles from step 3 on the white trapezoids.

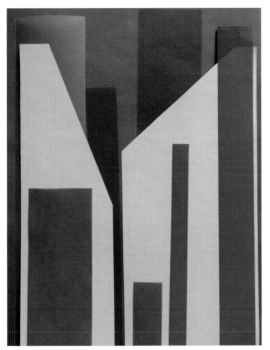

11 Place the 2 red rectangles from step 4 on the right white trapezoid.

12 Place the big green rectangle and yellow chamfered rectangle on the collage. These are the buildings. Then add 2 yellow rectangles as the billboards.

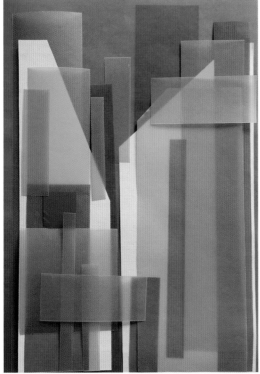

13 Place the small rectangles on the buildings as billboards.

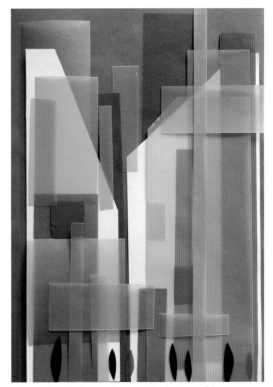

14 Place the human figures at the bottom of the background. Then properly add a few tracing paper rectangles to enhance the layering and enrich the collage. Adjust and set the overall layout.

5. Various Art Styles

Art style refers to the relatively consistent characteristic and tone of an artist or artistic group that are developed during a series of practices. In paper collage making, various art styles are widely applied. Here, we do not strictly follow the common art styles to define our paper collage works; but we can appreciate the different art styles when enjoying them: realism (see page 7) vs. freehand style, abstract expressionism vs. figurativism, eastern vs. western style, as well as fauvism and impressionism, etc. Different styles can provide us different feelings. Some artworks are like watercolor paintings (see page 23), some are like oil paintings, some are like traditional Chinese paintings, some are like prints, and so on.

The goal of developing art styles cannot be completely reached in one step. It requires us to understand and pay attention to them on a regular basis, learning how to apply them to different types of paper to fully integrate them. In this session, we will introduce four pieces of paper collages in different styles for studying purpose.

Flowers in a Vase (Gouache Painting Style)
Paper: embossed paper, printing paper, cardstock, and tissue
Dimensions: 40 × 40 cm
Gouache painting is a type of painting using a mixture of water and gouache paints to present the opaque and translucent effect which lies between oil painting and watercolor. This collage integrates the techniques of splitting, crumpling, and pinching and use high value of grayish paper to portray the opaque effect; whereas the use of white tissue paper fully illustrates the translucent effect.

Flowers in a Vase (Abstract Expressionism)

Abstract expressionism is a relative concept of figurativism. It extracts the commonality of the objects and integrates them to form a new concept. This collage *Flowers in a Vase* is composed of various bright pieces as the background with the simple, abstract, and colorful pieces as the flowers. Although it is not like drawing from life showing every single petal or pistil, it is still full of colors and visual impacts.

Paper: brownish yellow, violet, purple, white, red, dark brown, grass green, dark red, lemon, tangerine, navy blue, lake blue and pink embossed paper; yellow and black cardstock.
Background: white cardstock (25 × 25 cm).

1 Tear a few large pieces from the dark red, lemon, brownish yellow, and tangerine embossed paper as the scene at the back.

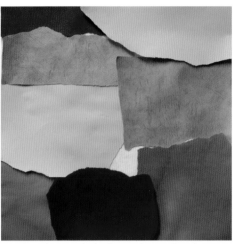

2 Place them on the background. Note the color coordination and combination.

3 Tear a trapezoid from the navy blue embossed paper and an irregular piece from the black cardstock.

4 Place these 2 pieces on the lower part of the picture as the vase and its shadow. Note that the vase is on top of the shadow.

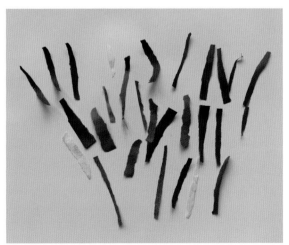

5 Tear a number of strips in different widths and lengths from various color paper.

6 Place the grass green, lake blue, and white strips on the left side of the vase as the patterns.

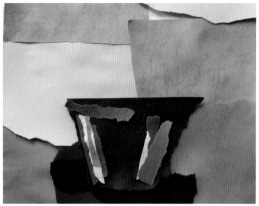

7 Add more strips of other colors on the right side of the vase.

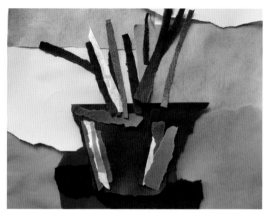

8 Place some strips of various colors on top of the vase as the stems. Note the tilted angles. These strips can be stems as well as the vase patterns. Don't you enjoy the freedom and flexibility of paper collage?

9 Continue to add more stems and let them "grow" outside the vase.

10 Tear a number of irregular pieces from various color paper as the petals.

11 Place the bigger petals on the stems and vase.

12 Continue to add the rest of the petals to form a luxurious picture. Some petals can be scattered at the background as the fallen ones. Adjust and set the overall layout.

Flowers in a Vase (Watercolor Style)

Following the rigid definition, watercolor is a painting method. For the purpose of introducing the flexibility and impressiveness of paper collage, we roughly classify it as an art style. Watercolor painting is illustrated by mixing water and paints, demonstrating the translucent and fluidity features to deliver fresh effects.

This art piece applies the method of watercolor but replaces the paints with color pieces, mimicking the brush strokes to provide a range of color scales. The light flowers are presented by thinner paper so that the darker color at the back can be shown. This meets the feature of watercolor as the paint is translucent, which is able to penetrate the colors underneath. The use of tracing paper, moreover, can promote the water effect. This artwork is luminous, lively, and full of harmony.

Paper: sand, brownish yellow, light ocher, dark brown, violet, purple, pink and gray embossed paper; light yellow and lavender printing paper; black and white cardstock; pink tracing paper.

Background: white cardstock (20 × 20 cm).

1 Tear a number of irregular pieces from various light color paper as the petals and leaves.

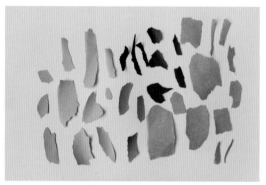

2 Tear a number of long and irregular pieces from various dark color paper as the vase shadow, stems and leaves.

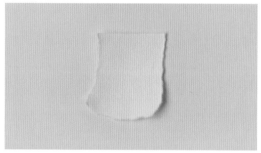

3 Tear a rectangle as shown from the white cardstock as the vase.

4 Tear a shadow as shown from the black cardstock.

5 Place the shadow on the lower part of the background.

6 Place the white vase and brownish yellow shadow that is casted on the wall onto the black shadow.

7 Scatter the large irregular gray and violet pieces as the background scene.

8 Place the large light ocher irregular pieces around the vase as leaves. Add the long light ocher pieces onto the vase as the stems.

9 Place the long pieces with dark color (black, gray, light ocher, lavender, etc.) on the vase and right side of the picture as the shadows.

10 Add the dark brown pieces on top of the vase as the leaves at the back.

11 Continue to add sand color petals onto the top right of the vase.

12 Place the pink petals on the top left.

13 Add the irregular purple pieces onto the left as the petals at the back.

14 Place several light yellow petals, overlapping each other, in the center to enhance the three-dimensional effect.

15 Tear a few long pieces from the pink tracing paper as to present the watercolor fluidic effect.

16 Scatter the pink tracing paper pieces around to make the work luminous. Adjust and set the overall layout.

Flowers in a Vase (Impressionism)

Impressionism is the epoch-making art movement in the western painting history. It came to prominence in 1880's and affected the whole world. The extensive strokes and play of light on objects are the main characteristics of impressionism.

This paper collage is derived from these two characteristics of impressionism. The vase and flowers are in arbitrary style without much embellishment. Regarding the colors, it conveys the seven colors of the spectrum (red, orange, yellow, green, blue, indigo and violet) forming a bright picture. It also makes use of the translucency of tracing paper to present the shadowy effect.

Paper: yellow, green and blue tracing paper; violet iridescent paper.
Background: white cardstock (20 × 30 cm).

1 Tear a vase from the blue tracing paper. You can draw the outline of a vase and cut it out using a knife to make it more precise.

2 Tear 3 irregular pieces from the blue tracing paper.

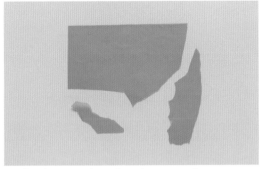

3 Tear 3 pieces as shown from the green tracing paper.

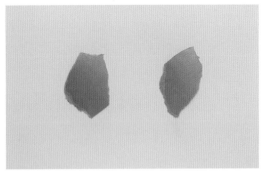

4 Tear 2 pieces from the violet iridescent paper.

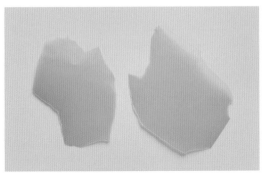

5 Tear 2 big pieces from the yellow tracing paper.

6 Tear several irregular pieces from the violet iridescent paper.

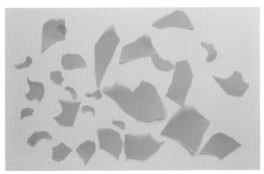

7 Tear a number of small irregular pieces from the yellow tracing paper.

8 Tear 3 small pieces from the green tracing paper as the leaves.

9 Place the blue vase at the bottom of the background. Place the blue pieces from step 2 on the background as the leaves at the back.

10 Place the green pieces from step 3 on the vase top, middle and bottom as the shadows of the leaves and flowers. Note the coordination between the different areas and different pieces.

11 Place the violet pieces from step 4 on the left side of the collage as the leaves.

12 Place the yellow pieces from step 5 above the vase as the flowers.

13 Scatter the smaller violet pieces from step 6 on the collage as the leaves.

14 Place the yellow pieces from step 7 one by one on the collage as the flowers. They can overlap one another.

15 Continue to add more yellow flowers.

16 Place the green pieces from step 8 at the lower part of the flowers like extruding out from the bouquet. Adjust and set the overall layout.

Flowers in a Vase (Freehand Brush Style)

After seeing a few *Flowers in a Vase* of different styles, let's see how to merge the freehand brush style into paper collage.

This artwork is created with magazine paper and embossed paper. First is to arrange the embossed paper as the background scenery. Then skillfully apply the magazine paper using its original graphics and colors to interpret the flowers and leaves. This art is in a freeform style. Its components are scattered but the concept is focused. Using magazine paper to fabricate the flowers can form a distinct lively scene.

From this we can see the diversity and arbitrary of the color and pattern of magazine paper. It can be transformed into whatever components that we need for our work. To create an outstanding paper collage, all we need is our imagination.

Paper: magenta, ultramarine, navy blue and violet embossed paper; magazine paper of various color.
Background: white cardstock (20 × 20 cm).
Tool: knife.

1 Tear a number of long irregular pieces from the navy blue embossed paper.

2 Vertically place the navy blue long pieces on the top part of the white background.

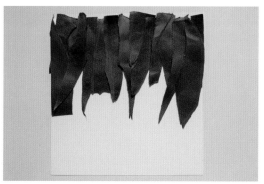

3 Continue to add more navy blue long pieces to fully cover the top part of the collage.

4 Add some navy blue long pieces to the lower part of the collage, having part of the white background exposed.

5 Tear a number of long irregular pieces from the ultramarine embossed paper.

6 Place the ultramarine pieces on the lower part of the collage to cover all the white space. The colors of top and bottom are similar but different, which can enhance the layering effect.

7 Tear a number of long irregular pieces from the dark part of the magazine paper. The magazine paper itself is in gradient colors which enrich the visual impact of the collage.

8 Place the large magazine pieces on the collage as the flower stems and leaves.

9 Continue to add the small long pieces as the leaves.

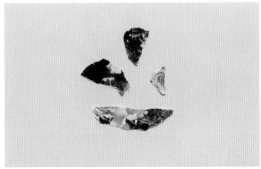

10 Tear a few irregular pieces from the green and pink magazine paper.

11 Place them under the stems and leaves as if they are scattered petals.

12 Tear several small irregular pieces from the violet embossed paper.

13 Scatter the violet pieces on the collage to enhance the color impact.

14 Tear a few long and small pieces from the magenta embossed paper.

15 Scatter the magenta pieces around to enrich the image.

16 Tear a few petals from the red dress of the magazine paper following the direction of the dress folds. You can see that the folds are like the texture of the petals.

17 Assemble the first flower using the red petals on the upper right of the collage.

18 Arrange the second flower on the lower left of the first flower. This flower is a bit smaller than the first one.

19 Construct 2 buds on the left and lower right of the first flower.

20 Adjust the overall layout, trim the edges with a knife, and set with glue.

6. Warm and Cold Colors

In visual arts, colors can be categorized as warm (red, orange, and yellow), cold (cyan and blue) and neutral (black, white, and gray) according to perceptual and psychological effects to the contrast. Warm colors provide an intimate feeling while cold colors deliver a sense of distance. The intensity of color is concluded from a long-time practice with imagination. Red, orange, and yellow relate to the sun and flames, producing a warm feeling and thus are classified as warm colors. Cyan and blue associate with the seas and sky, yielding a cold feeling and thus are categorized as cold colors. Black, white, and gray distribute a non-warm and non-cold feeling, and thus grouped as neutral.

Paintings usually makes full use of color theory, showing the color orientation. When we construct our paper collage, we can refer to this concept and choose the proper color tones to reflect the subjects and emotions. The options of colors are enormous. Through selection, combination, creativity, and imagination, unexpected results may come up.

For your reference, we will demonstrate two artworks separately using warm and cold colors to fully convey the themes.

The Desert
Paper: embossed paper, printing paper, and cardstock
Dimensions: 25 × 25 cm
This collage is based on the expressive freehand brush style, transforming and exaggerating the subjects to present the bleak scene of the desert. The cold colors set the art in a desolated tone, delivering the typical lonely feeling of Chinese poetry depicting frontier.

Chrysanthemums

Chrysanthemum represents faith, purity, beauty and grace in Chinese culture. These are the reasons why scholars and artists like to use chrysanthemums as the theme for their poems and paintings.

When chrysanthemum is presented in traditional Chinese paintings, artists have a tendency to use cold colors to emphasize its purity and grace. This collage, however, goes off the track, highlighting its warm and sunny attributes. The work utilizes a lot of warm colors, such as red, orange and yellow, to form an enthusiastic and gorgeous picture. This proves that even though the features of an object cannot be changed, one can still contribute his feelings through different tones, whether they conform to the object or not, to produce an unexpected result.

Paper: dark red, dark brown, black, sand, brownish yellow, tangerine, lemon and navy blue embossed paper; white cardstock.
Background: white cardstock (20 × 20 cm).

1 Tear 3 large pieces from brownish yellow, black, and navy blue embossed paper as the scene at the back.

2 Put together the 3 pieces on the white cardstock background as the scene at the back.

3 Tear 1 half-circular and 2 irregular pieces from the black embossed paper as the shadows.

4 Place the half-circular piece on the bottom of the picture as the vase. Then add the 2 irregular pieces onto the left as the shadows.

5 Tear a number of irregular pieces from the sand embossed paper.

6 Tear a number of irregular pieces from the dark brown embossed paper.

7 Tear a number of irregular pieces from the lemon embossed paper.

8 Tear a number of irregular pieces from the tangerine embossed paper.

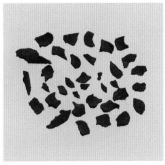

9 Tear a number of irregular pieces from the dark red embossed paper.

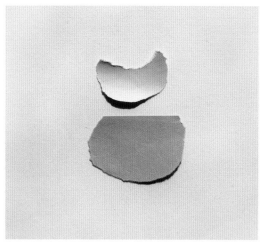

10 Tear a crescent from the white cardstock and a half-circle from the sand embossed paper.

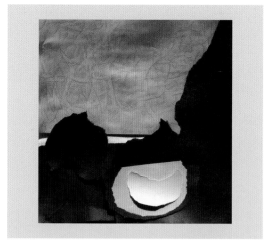

11 Place them on the black vase to reflect the contrast between light and shade under a light source.

12 Add the sand pieces above the vase as the receptacles. Note that their positions are where the chrysanthemums will be.

13 Continue to add more sand color receptacles onto the top part of the picture. Try to fill it up.

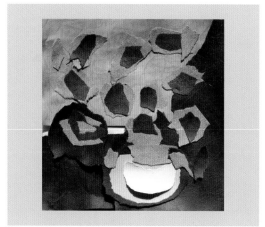

14 Add the dark brown pieces onto the sand color receptacles as the disc florets.

15 Place the lemon pieces around the dark brown disc florets at the lower left. This is the first row of the ray florets.

16 Repeat the previous step to arrange the other chrysanthemums.

17 Place the tangerine pieces around the chrysanthemum right above the vase. This is the second row of the ray florets.

18 Continue to add the tangerine pieces onto the chrysanthemums on the left and right as the second row of the ray florets.

19 Scatter the rest of the tangerine ray florets around the other disc florets. No need to arrange them in a row.

20 Put the dark red pieces around the chrysanthemums on top. This is the third row of the ray florets.

21 Continue to add the dark red pieces. The lower the location, the less the pieces. Adjust and set the overall layout.

Daffodils

Chinese daffodil is a variant of French narcissus introduced from Italy in Tang dynasty more than one thousand years ago. Different from the western culture, daffodil is a symbol of purity, unity, and auspiciousness in Chinese culture; and therefore, people like to have some at home in Chinese New Year.

   The main color of this artwork is blue. Together with other colors, violet, green, white, and black, this piece of art successfully highlights the purity and grace of daffodil. Feel free to compare with the previous lesson *Chrysanthemums*, which is in the warm tone, to experience applications of different color tones in paper collage making.

Paper: black, navy blue, violet, dark green, emerald and blackish green embossed paper; lake blue, white, purple, lemon and sand printing paper.
Background: black embossed paper (20 × 20 cm).

1 Tear the pieces as shown using the lake blue printing paper, violet and navy blue embossed paper as the background scene.

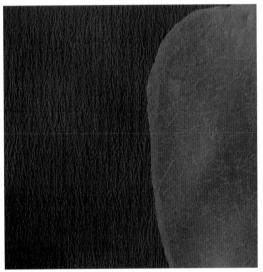

2 Place the navy blue piece on the black background. Note that the right edge of the navy blue piece aligns with the background edge.

3 Add the other 2 pieces as the background scene.

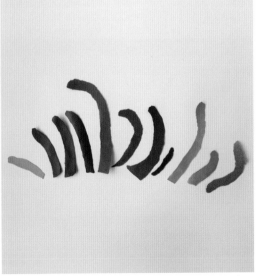

4 Tear several J-shaped pieces as shown from various color paper as the stems and leaves of the daffodils.

5 Place the 2 longest navy blue J-shaped pieces on the left side of the picture.

6 Continue to add more J-shaped pieces of other colors around. Note that the stems and leaves are facing different directions.

7 Place more J-shaped pieces of different colors on top.

8 Tear some irregular pieces from the violet and blackish green embossed paper as well as the lake blue and purple printing paper.

9 Add the violet irregular pieces to enrich the styles of stems and leaves.

10 Place the blackish green and lake blue irregular pieces around to enhance the layering effect.

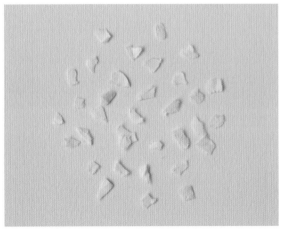

11 Tear a number of small pieces from the white printing paper.

12 Arrange the white pieces as the flowers and scatter them on the top half of the collage. Note that the flowers are in different styles.

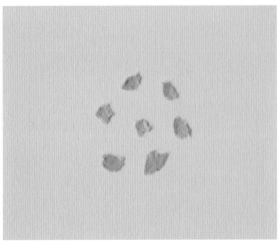

13 Tear a few irregular pieces from the sand printing paper.

14 Add the sand color pieces on top of the white flowers as the coronas.

15 Tear several smaller pieces from the lemon printing paper.

16 Add the lemon pieces in the center of the flowers as the inner coronas. Adjust and set the overall layout.

7. Freehand Brush Style

Freehand brush style is one of the traditional Chinese painting techniques. Different from *gongbi* style, it does not concentrate on the details. Instead, it emphasizes on conveying the artist's feelings and the subject's meanings, simplifying the image but enriching the implications. Freehand brush style is also known as "idea sketching." In the ancient Chinese poetry, poets sometimes pushed aside the detailed descriptions and simply pointed out the main features of the subjects and the surrounding environment to elevate a specific atmosphere, using the subjects and scenery as a tool to express the theme and concept.

Due to the limitations of paper and techniques, paper collage is not able to describe details as *gongbi* style. It, however, provides more possibilities to convey ideas in the freehand brush style. This is very important to art creation. The randomness and flexibility of paper collage freely allow us to use paper to present the subject. All in all, paper collage encourages unrestrained imaginations and styles.

Paper collage emphasizes on the resemblance of spirit but not form and shape. As long as the concept can be delivered, the collage artwork is considered as a successful one. There is no need to adhere to our methods and lessons during your creative production. Feel free and be bold to create with your personal idea and power. With continuous improvement, you will be able to fully express your ideas and thoughts.

The Three Gorges
Paper: embossed paper, printing paper, and sketch paper
Dimensions: 54 × 39 cm
The Three Gorges (Qutang Groge, Wu Gorge and Xiling Gorge) near the Yangtze River is one of the scenic landmarks in China. Referring to the traditional Chinese landscape painting, this collage is constructed by the crumpling and pinching techniques to present the magnificent canyons and mountains, leaving the empty space in the middle as the Yangtze River. Only three colors are selected in the whole artwork and yet successfully deliver the majestic scene.

Morning Glory

"Fall is the season for chrysanthemums; winter is the season for plum blossoms; spring is the time for Chinese flowering crabapple; winter is the time for morning glories." In China, morning glory is the essential flower in summer. It is a popular theme in ancient poems as well as traditional paintings. The flower is beautiful but not delicate. It is not afraid of the hot summer. It blooms when roosters start to crow. This makes it a symbol of hard-working.

This artwork uses the freehand brush style of morning glory in traditional Chinese painting as a reference, replacing brush strokes with paper pieces to portray the scene of twining vines and flower blooming. The color change of the leaves and vines is presented like a brush stroke, gradually stretching from dark to light. This collage has a very classic and elegant color combination, presenting simplicity with a profound artistic concept.

Paper: pink, violet, light blue, black and various shades of gray embossed paper.
Background: gray cardstock (10% grayscale, 20 × 20 cm).
Tools: scissors.

1 Tear an irregular piece from the medium gray embossed paper.

2 Tear 2 irregular pieces from the dark gray embossed paper.

3 Tear 3 small pieces from the light gray embossed paper as the leaves.

4 Tear 3 small pieces from the light blue embossed paper as the leaves.

5 Tear a few long pieces from the black embossed paper.

6 Tear a few long pieces from the pink embossed paper.

7 Tear a number of long pieces from the violet embossed paper.

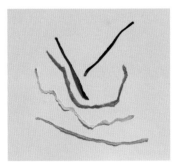

8 Tear some long, thin, curl, and irregular pieces from various gray embossed paper as the vines.

9 Cut several comma-shaped pieces from the black embossed paper as the sepals of morning glory.

10 Place the medium gray piece onto the center of the background. Then add 1 dark gray piece on top and the other dark gray piece on the right. These are the leaves.

11 Place the 3 small light grey leaves below the big leaves. Note the gap in between.

12 Place the light blue leaves on top of the light gray leaves.

13 Add some black long pieces vertically onto the dark gray leaf on the lower right. The black long pieces are like pure ink on Chinese painting without using water to dilute.

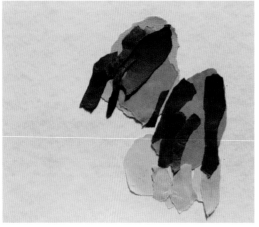

14 Continue to add the black long pieces on top of the dark gray leaf. Note the direction and correlation of the pieces to deliver the gradual color change of Chinese painting.

15 Add some small black pieces on top of the 2 dark gray leaves as the dotting brush strokes. Dotting is a Chinese painting technique using irregular dots to depict leaves, rocks, etc.

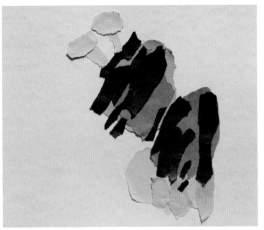

16 Put the pink pieces onto the top part of the collage as the crowns of the morning glories. Note the shape of the flowers, which has a wider top.

17 Place the violet pieces on top of the pink crowns as the petals of the 2 morning glories.

18 Scatter the violet pieces around as the buds.

19 Add the vines starting from the bottom of the collage to the buds.

20 Continue to add the vines. Note the vines of different gray values cross with each other.

21 Place the black sepals onto the connection point of the vines and buds. Adjust and set the overall layout.

The Warm Sun

Above the unlimited land, the red woodland together with the warm sun establish a spectacular natural scene. This piece of art tends not to outline the forest and sun. Instead, it delivers rough and carefree scene through the flexible paper collage. When we enjoy this artwork, the use of various warm colors seems to direct us to the gorgeous sunlight and give us comfort.

Nothing is very clear on this collage; but it successfully conveys the theme and message. This is a good example of using freehand brush style on paper collage.

Paper: brownish yellow, ocher, dark red, dark brown, pale yellow and pink embossed paper; tangerine cardstock.
Background: tangerine cardstock (20 × 20 cm).

1 Tear 2 large rectangular pieces from the dark brown embossed paper.

2 Tear 1 big and 1 small long pieces from the ocher embossed paper as the background scene and shadow.

3 Tear a few pieces in different sizes and shapes from the pink, pale yellow, and brownish yellow embossed paper.

4 Place the dark brown pieces on the tangerine background as the land. Note the connection of the 2 pieces.

5 Place the ocher background scene on the right as the woodland. Add the ocher shadow onto the land.

6 Place the largest pale yellow piece on the right side of the center as the large tree crown.

7 Add the 3 smaller pale yellow pieces on the left of the large tree crown as the small tree crowns.

8 Continue to add the brownish yellow pieces as the tree crowns to enrich the collage.

9 Place the pink piece on the left to enhance the color effect.

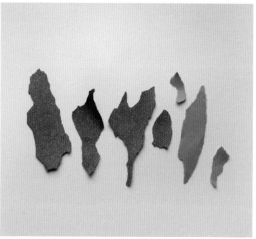

10 Tear a few free style pieces from the dark red embossed paper and tangerine cardstock.

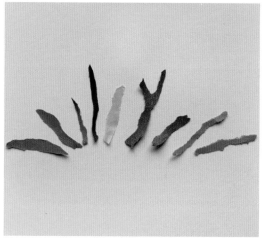

11 Tear several long pieces from various color paper.

12 Place the dark red pieces on top of the crowns as the branches and leaves.

13 Continue to add more pieces of other colors on top as the branches and leaves.

14 Add the tangerine pieces as the branches and leaves. The front view blends well with the background since the color is the same.

15 Tear a number of small pieces from the dark red and dark brown cardstock.

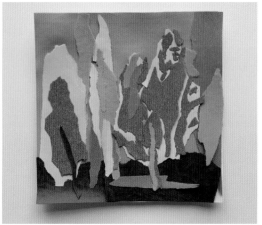

16 Add the dark red pieces onto the tree on the right side as the leaves to enhance the three-dimensional and layering effects.

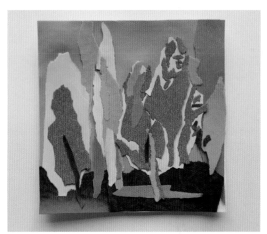

17 Add the small dark brown pieces to enrich the collage.

18 Tear 3 round pieces in different sizes from the pale yellow and brownish yellow embossed paper.

19 Stack the 3 round pieces to form the sun on top. Note that the outer circle is the lightest in color as the halo. Adjust and set the overall layout.

CHAPTER FOUR
Advanced Lessons

In the Introductory Lessons, we have systematically presented the common features of paper collage and the techniques of forming artistic styles. You should have learned a lot from the practices.

In these coming Advanced Lessons, we have selected some special artworks to illustrate the diversity and creativity of paper collage. Compare to the Introductory Lessons, the advanced ones are bigger with more techniques and deeper artistic concepts. After the in-depth study, we hope you can consolidate all the key points, gradually develop your own style and create remarkable paper collages.

In this chapter, *Craggy Rocks*, *The Cabins in the Woods*, *The Mandarin Fishes*, *The Chicken*, *Snow*, *Hanshan Temple* and *Woods* are collages that were made long time ago. Please compare the first image with the last one in the lessons, you will find the dissimilarities between the two.

The Little Town after a Snow
Paper: embossed paper, printing paper, cardstock, tissue, crepe paper and sketch paper
Dimensions: 54 × 39 cm
This paper collage depicts a scene of a town after a snow by referring to an abstract style. The extensive use of white sketch paper and crepe paper replicates the accumulated snow while the tissue covered on the roof and ground mimics the scene of snowmelt on a clear day.

1. The Good Companions

According to Chinese art culture, painting with flower, bird, fish or insect as the subject is called bird-and-flower painting. There are three styles: *gongbi*, freehand brush, and *gongbi* with freehand brush. *Gongbi* bird-and-flower painting is characterized by outlining the objects and brushing with layers of various shades. Freehand brush bird-and-flower painting, on the other hand, is based on simple and general style to depict the objects. The former one aims at preciseness while the latter one focuses on artistic expression. Paper collage is more fit for mimicing the freehand brush bird-and-flower painting.

This artwork vividly illustrates a pair of birds that are attached to one another by referring to the freehand brush style. Combined with watercolor painting techniques, it breaks through the traditional Chinese painting style. The fusion of the eastern and western painting styles makes the collage more unique.

Paper: brownish yellow, violet, dark red, light gray, medium gray and black embossed paper; lake blue, sky blue, light green, light yellow and pink printing paper.

Background: white sketch paper (30 × 40 cm).

1 Tear the heads of the 2 birds from the black embossed paper.

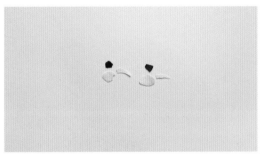

2 Tear the eyes from the black embossed paper and the beaks from the light yellow printing paper.

3 Assemble the 2 heads in the center of the background. Note the angle and gesture of the birds.

4 Tear the wing feathers of the 2 birds from the medium gray and dark red embossed paper. Note that the shape of the feather can affect the gesture of the birds. Thus, it can be a bit round to echo the chubbiness.

5 Place the medium gray feathers on the left bird.

6 Tear a few irregular pieces from the pink and light green printing paper as the breast and belly feathers of the 2 birds.

7 Add the pink piece onto the left bird as the belly feathers.

8 Tear several pieces in different sizes from the black embossed paper as the wing and thigh feathers of the 2 birds.

9 Place the black feathers on the left bird. Be sure to leave the medium gray edge as if it is the shading of the brush painting.

10 Add the dark red and black wing feathers to the right bird.

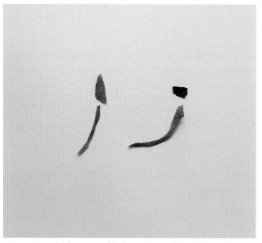

11 Tear the breast and belly outlines of the 2 birds from the medium gray and black embossed paper.

12 Place the breast and belly outlines below the heads.

13 Add the light green breast and belly feathers onto the 2 birds.

14 Add the black thigh feathers onto the 2 birds.

15 Tear a number of small irregular pieces from various color paper as the feathers of different parts.

16 Add the feathers of different colors onto the wings of the 2 birds. Note the direction of the feathers; for example, the feathers on the tail of the left bird slopes downwards or else it will look disorganized.

17 Continue to add the colorful feathers onto different parts of the birds.

18 Tear a number of long pieces from the light gray embossed paper, sky blue and light green printing paper as the background scene.

19 Place the light green and sky blue background components on the left side of the left bird. Be sure to mimic the brushstrokes of watercolor painting.

20 Add the light gray background components around the 2 birds. Adjust and set the overall layout.

2. Gateway

The gateway is one of the traditional Chinese architectural structures. The first one was built in the Zhou dynasty (1046–256 BC) to commend for filial piety. They can also be found in gardens, temples, palaces, mausoleums, and streets. Gateway is a tall structure with pillars and arches, usually constructed with wood, stone, brick, and glass, and located at the entrances. In Beijing, the capital of China, different types of gateways can be found along streets and alleys. Walking pass by them is like traveling back to the pass.

This collage captures the features of the traditional gateway, using the freehand brush style to illustrate the lintels, pillars, and inscribed tablet. Also having watercolor painting as a reference, this artwork refreshes the traditional Chinese color usage. The big red lantern polishes the whole picture and enhances the Chinese flavor.

Paper: sand, light ocher, ocher, dark brown, light gray, dark gray, purple and red embossed paper; black and tangerine cardstock.
Background: white sketch paper (30 × 40 cm).

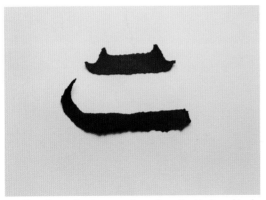

1 Tear the roof and upturned eave from the black cardstock.

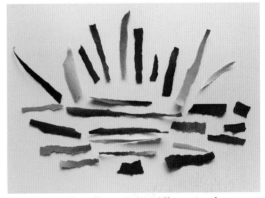

2 Tear a number of long pieces in different sizes from various color paper.

3 Tear a few thicker long pieces from various color paper.

4 Tear a few rectangles from various color paper.

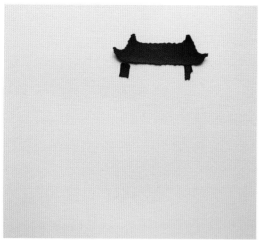

5 Place the roof of the gateway on top right of the background.

6 Place the upturned eave below the roof.

7 Add the pieces from steps 2 and 3 in the middle as the pillars and lintels.

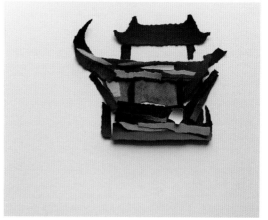

8 Continue to add the pillars and lintels. Note the color combination and overlapping.

9 Add the rectangular pieces from step 4 onto the top and middle of the gateway.

10 Place the thick long piece as the base pillars and ground.

11 Tear a big rectangle from the ocher embossed paper.

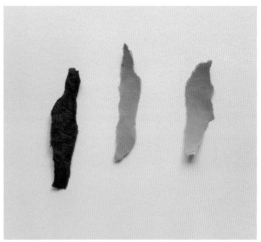

12 Tear 3 human figures from the dark brown embossed paper and tangerine cardstock.

13 Place the big ocher rectangular piece between the 2 pillars as the distant background scene. Add more pieces as the lintels, pillars, and the horizontal tablet.

14 Place the human figures next to the pillars as they are walking pass by the gateway.

15 Tear several long pieces from the black cardstock, light gray and dark gray embossed paper.

16 Tear the lantern components from the red embossed paper.

17 Add the black and dark gray pieces from step 15 to the left of the gateway as houses next to it.

18 Continue to add the light gray pieces from step 15 to describe the weathered walls. Although this is only a partial of the house, it represents the whole. This is also a form of artistic expression.

19 Assemble the round lantern body on the left of the gateway.

20 Add the tassels to the top and bottom of the lantern. Adjust and set the overall layout.

3. Craggy Rocks

This collage is composed by three and only three pieces of different color paper and skillfully portrays the two craggy rocks. The artist invented the "rubbing" technique and utilized the characteristics of paper to illustrate the gullies and veins of the rocks, fully demonstrating the freehand brush style in paper collage art. The composition looks simple and yet contains a great artistic concept, showing the artist's unique skill and painstaking effort to create collage.

Paper: sand embossed paper and white crepe paper.
Background: black cardstock (54 × 39 cm).

1 Tear a craggy rock from the sand embossed paper. Note the rough edges.

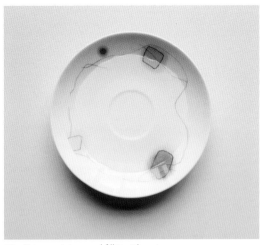

2 Get a container and fill it with water.

3 Tip your finger with water and rub the right side of the craggy rock. Some crumbs will come off from the surface.

4 Hold the craggy rock up against the light and you can see that the right side becomes thinner and translucent. This is the gully of the rock.

5 Continue to rub the middle to form more gullies and veins.

6 You can also "split" the surface of the paper to expose the rough texture.

7 Use both rubbing and splitting techniques to process the left side of the craggy rock.

8 The sand color craggy rock is done. You can see the irregular gullies and veins of the craggy rock from the picture.

9 Follow the previous steps to work on the white crepe paper to create the white craggy rock.

10 Place the white craggy rock on the left side of the black background. You will notice that the background color seeps through the thinned gullies and veins to form a special visual effect.

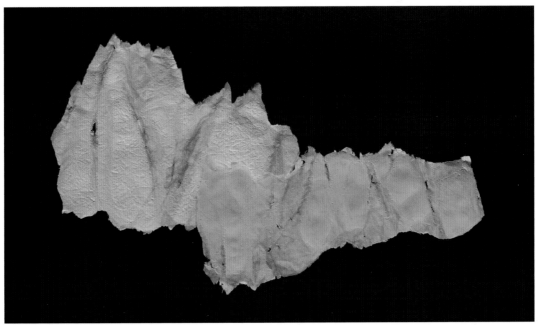

11 Partially overlap the white craggy rock with the sand craggy rock. Properly arrange the 2 pieces and set with glue.

4. The Cabins in the Woods

In the luxuriant foliage of the woods, here it restfully stands two simple cabins. This is a scene of comfort and harmony.

This piece of art consists of various bright colors that are boldly arranged to catch the audiences' eye. With the exception of the trunk, all other elements, such as the cabins, are made of large colorful scraps. They are mingled together to provide a strong visual impact and yet keep the harmony without a sense of vulgarity.

Paper: ivory, dark brown, ocher, magenta and violet embossed paper; orange-red, yellow and light gray cardstock.
Background: light gray cardstock (20 × 20 cm).
Tool: knife.

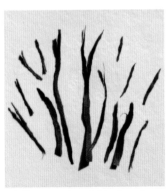

1 Tear out 2 sets of wall and roof pieces from the ivory and dark brown embossed paper. One is larger than the other to enhance the sense of perspective.

2 Tear some larger strips from the violet, ocher, and dark brown embossed paper as well as the orange-red cardstock.

3 Tear some strips from the magenta and ivory embossed paper as well as the orange-red cardstock similar to those in step 2 but smaller in size.

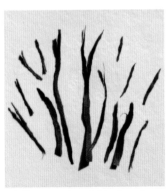

4 Tear a number of strips from the dark brown embossed paper in different lengths and widths as the trunks and branches.

5 Randomly tear some small pieces using the yellow and orange-red cardstock.

6 Tear some rectangular pieces from the dark brown, ocher, and magenta embossed paper as well as the light gray cardstock as the doors and windows.

7 Cut some thin strips from the orange-red cardstock as the window frames.

8 Tear a number of small pieces from the ocher embossed paper as defoliation.

9 Tear a few strips from the light gray cardstock.

10 Place the dark brown roofs on top of the walls.

11 Locate the cabins on the lower center of the background.

12 Vertically place the strips from step 2 onto the right side of the background as the tree crowns.

13 Continue to add more strips on the left of the background above the roofs as the tree crowns.

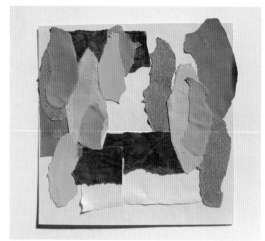

14 Overlap the tree crowns with the strips from step 3 to enhance the layering effect.

15 Place the long and broad strips from step 4 onto the tree crowns as the trunks.

16 Continue to add the smaller ones as the branches.

17 Place the orange-red pieces from step 5 onto the trees and roofs.

18 Continue to add the yellow pieces from step 5 to enhance the picture.

19 Place the rectangular pieces and thin strips from steps 6 and 7 onto the cabins as the doors and windows. They can be in a casual style.

20 Place the small pieces from step 8 below the cabins.

21 Add the strips from step 9 onto the bottom of the collage as the ground. Adjust and secure the overall layout.

5. The Mandarin Fishes

The mandarin fish is very popular in China due to its refreshing deliciousness. Since mandarin fish in Chinese (*gui*, 鳜) is a homophone of rich (*gui*, 贵), this fish is a symbol of wealth.

This collage refers to *The Song of a Fisherman* by Zhang Zhihe (732–774), a poet of the Tang dynasty:

The white egrets fly over the western mountains,
The mandarin fishes swim under the peach blossoms.
With bamboo rain hat and straw cape in green,
Need not to return even in rain and wind.

   Although the background is quite blank with only a few leaves,
this collage truly captures the scenery of the poem. The two yellowish
brown mandarin fishes vividly swimming under the peach tree lead you to think of the
fisherman wearing a green bamboo rain hat and straw cape on the shore. The grayish and
brownish pieces masterly stimulate the tonality of traditional Chinese painting, enriching
the three-dimensional effect of the fishes and layering effect of the picture.

Paper: sand, white and black cardstock; light gray, medium gray and light ocher embossed
paper.
Background: white cardstock (20 × 20 cm).

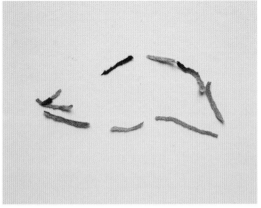

1 Tear a number of strips from various color paper as the
outline of the mandarin fish. Tear 2 small round pieces
from the black cardstock as the eyes.

2 Arrange the strips to form the lips of the first fish on the
left.

3 Continue to arrange the strips to finish the outline. Note
the use of different color to mimic the shading of ink-wash
painting.

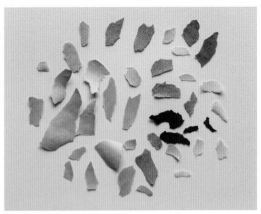

4 Tear a number of irregular pieces in different sizes from
various color paper as the fish patterns.

5 Arrange the patterns of the left fish head using the small irregular pieces. They can overlap one another to simulate the mixing of ink and water, and different brush strokes in Chinese painting.

6 Arrange the patterns of the fish body using the large and light color irregular pieces.

7 Arrange the tail with more pieces.

8 Place 2 big light gray pieces above the first fish head as the patterns of the second fish.

9 Place some long pieces below the pieces of step 8 to outline the head of the second fish. Note that the second fish faces upward.

10 Continue to add some small irregular pieces onto the second fish head.

11 Arrange the dorsal fin of the first fish using irregular pieces.

12 Assemble the pelvic and pectoral fins of the second fish below the first fish as one fish overlaps the other.

13 Tear a number of long pieces from the light ocher embossed paper and black cardstock as the branches and leaves at the back.

14 Arrange clusters of light ocher branches and leaves and place on the top right, to simulate the light shades of Chinese painting.

15 Add some black branches and leaves onto the left of the light ocher ones to simulate the dark shades of Chinese painting.

16 Add the eyes for both fishes. Adjust and set the overall layout.

6. The Chicken

This collage is one of a kind, using the special texture of tissue to simulate the feather fluffiness. The form of the chicken is referred to the freehand brush style of Chinese traditional bird-and-flower painting. Although there is no define outlines and strokes, the chubby chicken is thoroughly presented. Meanwhile, the beak and toes are created in a more precise method. The different techniques are skillfully used to vividly display the naive chicken.

The main portion of this collage is the tangerine background, leaving large blank space. On the contrary, the main element is relatively small and located at the lower part of the collage. This creates an ethereal style showing an exquisite artistic beauty.

Paper: dark brown embossed paper; light yellow printing paper; white tissue.
Background: tangerine printing paper (21 × 30 cm).
Tool: scissors.

1 Tear the body, head and wings of the chicken from the tissue. The parts can be arbitrary and distinguished by different sizes.

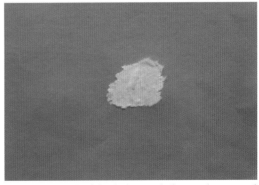

2 Place the body of the chicken on the lower right corner of the background.

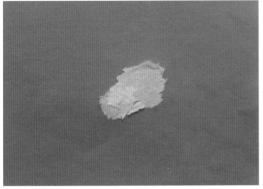

3 Add the head on the left side of the body. The 2 parts overlap each other so that the intersection is more natural.

4 Place the left wing on the body near the back of the head.

5 Tear a small piece from the tissue to cover the tail.

6 Tear another small tissue piece to cover the head. We need to construct several layers of tissue to emphasize the main parts of the chicken.

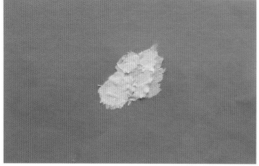

7 Add the right wing above the body.

8 Place a small tissue piece below the body as the left thigh.

9 Use a pair of scissors to cut a small triangle and a few strips from the light yellow printing paper as the beak, shanks and toes.

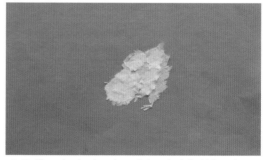

10 Place the shank and toes below the left thigh as shown.

11 Place the other toes below the right thigh. Note that the right leg does not have a shank to distinguish the front and rear positions so that it looks more realistic.

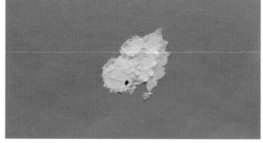

12 Add the beak onto the head. Tear a small dot from the dark brown embossed paper as the eye and place it on the right side of the head. The chicken that is pecking the stuff on the ground is complete. Adjust and set the overall layout.

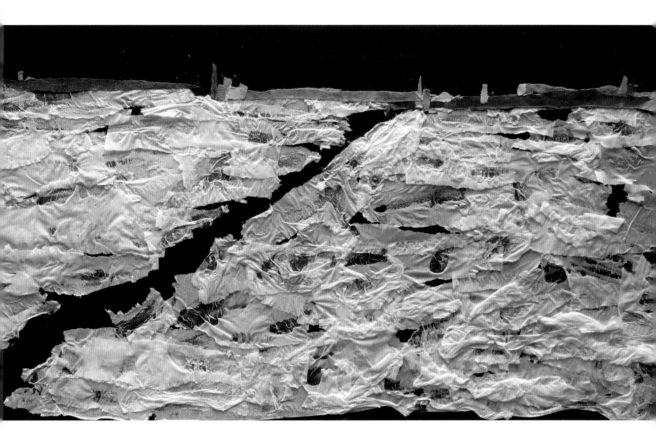

7. Snow

This piece of art is made of tissue with various techniques, truly demonstrating the diversity of tissue presentation in paper collage. The overlapping layers of tissue ingeniously exhibit the depth of the snow, whereas the softness of the material makes the collage surface fluffy like cotton, properly depicting the characteristics of snow. Also, the black background has a high contrast against the white snow which creates a substantial visual impact. The uncovered portion forms a clear path where snow has been removed. The path coordinates with the buildings from afar forming a meaningful scene. This paper collage performs the innovated ideas and new explorations.

Paper: navy blue, ultramarine, violet and gray embossed paper; lake blue, sky blue and orange-red printing paper; white tissue.
Background: black cardstock (60 × 30 cm).
Tools: glue and brush.

1 Tear a few strips from the lake blue printing paper, navy blue and gray embossed paper.

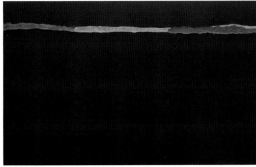

2 Connect the strips on top of the background. This is the horizon. Note the color arrangement.

3 Tear several small irregular pieces from various color paper.

4 Place these small pieces above the horizon as the high-rises from afar. Note that each group of pieces has a different density to reflect the building clusters in the real world.

5 Tear several strips from the tissue.

6 Place the tissue on the right below the horizon.

7 Pinch the tissue to form creases.

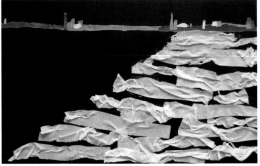

8 Continue to add tissue to form a trapezoid as the snow.

9 We can also crumple the tissue, unfold, and place it on the snow.

10 Or we can put some glue on the black background among the tissue pieces.

11 Then place the tissue on the glue.

12 The tissue becomes transparent and discloses the black background.

13 We can also tip the glue with a brush and then sweep the edges of the tissue to enhance the creases.

14 Tear a few small tissue pieces and place them on the snow to fully cover the black background.

15 Repeat the steps to add the tissue onto the left side of the collage.

16 Fully cover the triangular snow area on the left with tissue. Adjust and set the overall layout.

8. Hanshan Temple

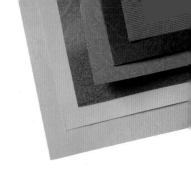

When the moon sets, crows caw, frost lingers all over the sky,
Maples and fishermen's lights by the river hear my sleepless sigh.
Beyond the city of Suzhou where Hanshan Temple left in the cold,
Midnight bell in the lonely night shatters all the way to my boat.

This is a far-famed poem *A Night Mooring by Maple Bridge* by Zhang Ji, a poet of the Tang dynasty. He traveled to Hanshan Temple in Suzhou after the An Lushan Rebellion and composed this poem to express his worries about the country during the time of trouble.

The artist of this collage captures the poet's intents, such as night, moon, and boat, and creates in the freehand style. The withered plantains in the front, desolated boat in the middle, temple from afar, and lonely moon in the sky properly portray the distressed atmosphere. The black background further intensifies the distressed theme, emphasizing the quietude.

Paper: peach, pale yellow, blackish green, lake blue, navy blue and violet embossed paper.
Background: black cardstock (20 × 40 cm).

1 Tear a few pieces from the violet embossed paper as the components of mountains, plantains, and temple.

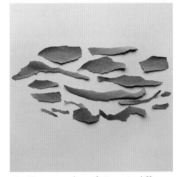

2 Tear a number of pieces in different sizes and shapes from the lake blue embossed paper as the plantain stems and leaves.

3 Tear a number of pieces in different sizes and shapes from the blackish green embossed paper as the plantain stems and leaves.

4 Tear a few pieces from the navy blue embossed paper as the components of the river, boat, and plantains.

5 Tear 2 round pieces from the pale yellow and peach embossed paper. The former one is a bit smaller than the latter one.

6 Place the violet mountains on the lower part of the background. The uneven edge on top is like the continuous landscape from afar.

7 Place the navy blue river and boat below the mountains.

8 Add a few long lake blue and navy blue pieces onto the lower right as the roots of the plantains.

9 Continue to add the longer lake blue pieces above the roots as the stems.

10 Place the blackish green and violet pieces around the lake blue stems to enhance the layering effect.

11 Add the large navy blue pieces above the stems as the leaf.

12 Add 3 lake blue leaves above the navy blue leaf. Note the layout, space, and directions.

13 Continue to add some small lake blue leaves that overlaps each other to enhance the three-dimensional effect.

14 Place the blackish green leaves on top to enrich the colors.

15 Place small leaves of various color among the other leaves to display the distressed atmosphere.

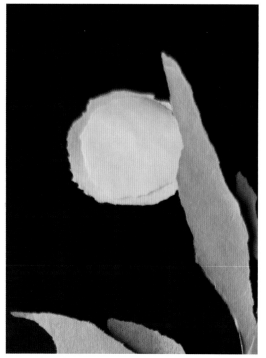

16 Place the peach moon above the plantains. It is partially covered by a leaf to emphasize the sentiment. Add the pale yellow round piece on top of the peach moon. The peach part exposed is like the halo around the moon.

17 Place the violet temple components above the mountains. Adjust and set the overall layout.

9. Woods

This collage refers to the coloring technique of impressionism, having a lot of bright and saturated colors to depict the woods under sunlight and reflect the shadowing effect on the trees. The overlapping technique is elaborately used, with the paper pieces occupying the main portion of the picture, leaving almost no blank space. This highly illustrates the luxuriance of the leaves. The mingling of colors and gradient of shades effectively enhance the picture, showing an intensified, scattered, and yet not disorganized effect.

Paper: dark brown, dark gray, brown, brownish yellow, grayish green and navy blue embossed paper; tangerine, yellow, light yellow, pink, orange-red, red, dark red, violet and lavender printing paper.
Background: white cardstock (39 × 54 cm).
Tool: knife.

1 Tear a number of long pieces from the darker tone paper.

2 Place them on the bottom of the background as the ground. Note the overlapping and intersecting of different color pieces.

3 Continue to add the long pieces to cover up the ground.

4 Tear several irregular pieces from the grayish green embossed paper as the leaves.

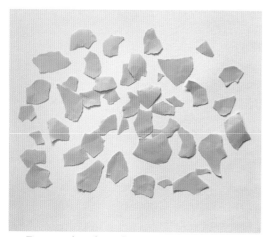

5 Tear a number of irregular pieces from the yellow printing paper as the leaves.

6 Add the grayish green leaves onto the lower part of the collage. Note the leaf layout. Place the yellow leaves on the grayish green leaves.

7 Tear a number of irregular pieces from the light yellow printing paper as the leaves.

8 Place the light yellow leaves on the yellow leaves.

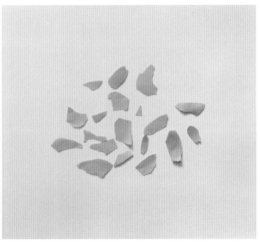

9 Tear a number of irregular pieces from the tangerine and yellow printing paper as the leaves.

10 Place the tangerine and yellow leaves on the light yellow leaves.

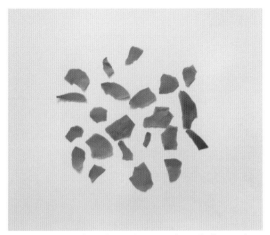

11 Tear a number of irregular pieces from the brownish yellow embossed paper as the leaves.

12 Place the brownish yellow leaves on the tangerine and yellow leaves. Note that the brownish yellow leaves are gathered in the center.

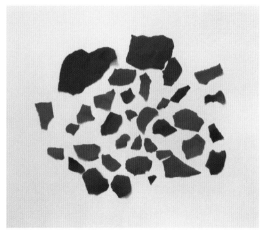

13 Tear a number of irregular pieces from the orange-red, red and dark red printing paper as the leaves. A few of them are to be in bigger sizes.

14 Place the reddish leaves on the yellowish leaves that are on the top part so that it creates a gradient effect—colors gradually darken as going upwards.

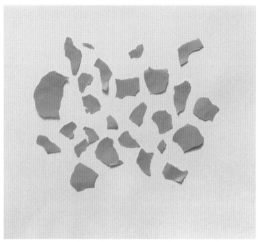

15 Tear a number of irregular pieces from the pink printing paper as the leaves.

16 Place the pink leaves on the woods. Be sure to scatter them among the reddish and yellowish leaves.

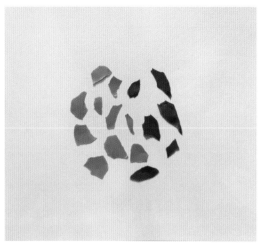

17 Tear a number of irregular pieces from the lavender and violet printing paper as the leaves.

18 Scatter the lavender and violet leaves in the woods to enhance the collage.

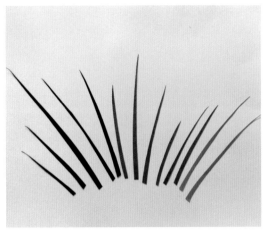

19 Use a knife to cut long pieces from the dark brown, brown and brownish yellow embossed paper as the trunks.

20 Group the trunks of various colors on the right. Note that different colors are to be alternating.

21 Add a group of trunks on the left.

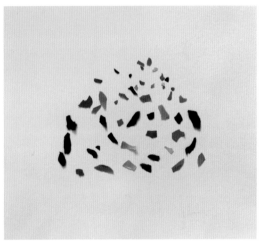

22 Tear a number of small pieces from various color paper.

23 Scatter them on the woods.

24 Place some small pieces on top of the trees to depict the scene of leaves blowing in the wind. Adjust and set the overall layout.

10. Clouds Floating in the Mountains

Chinese landscape painting is a traditional painting style that depicts natural scenery such as mountains and rivers. Fully developed in the Tang dynasty, it reached its peak in the Song dynasty (960–1279) and became the mainstream of traditional Chinese painting.

This collage makes use of paper to substitute for brushstrokes to illustrate a beautiful scene. The artist skillfully practices the crumpling and pinching techniques to transform paper into three-dimensional artwork. He also selects different types of paper such as embossed paper and crepe paper to simulate the brushstrokes of Chinese landscape painting to vividly present the overlapping mountains. The softness and translucency of tissue is truly fit to show the features of clouds and mist. With the freehand brush style and excellent composition, this art highly exhibits the diversity of paper collage.

Paper: grass green, dark green, emerald, sky blue, light blue, dark gray, grayish green and black embossed paper; light gray and pastel green printing paper; white crepe paper; white tissue.
Background: white cardstock (60 × 50 cm).

1 Tear a few pieces as shown from the dark gray embossed paper, pastel green and light gray printing paper.

2 Place them on the center of the background as the background scene.

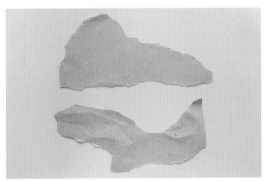

3 Tear 2 big mountains from the grayish green embossed paper.

4 Place the grayish green mountains on the top part of the background as the mountains from afar.

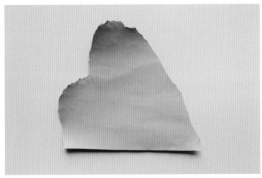

5 Tear another mountain from the light gray printing paper.

6 Crumple the piece.

7 Pinch the paper to form creases like the uneven texture of the rock and mountain to enhance the three-dimensional effect.

8 Fold the edges backwards to form smooth outlines. Make another mountain by repeating the above steps.

9 Place the first mountain on the center of the collage.

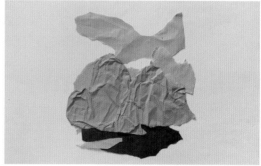

10 Overlap the first mountain by the second mountain.

11 Tear 2 long pieces from the black embossed paper and white crepe paper.

12 Refer to steps 5 to 8, create 3 other mountains from the dark gray embossed paper using pinching, crumpling, and folding.

13 Refer to steps 5 to 8 again to create a grass green mountain.

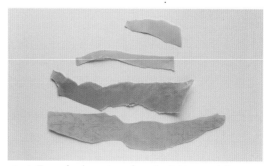

14 Tear a few long pieces from the light gray printing paper, sky blue and light blue embossed paper as the river.

15 You can use the splitting technique to process the edges to simulate the translucency of water.

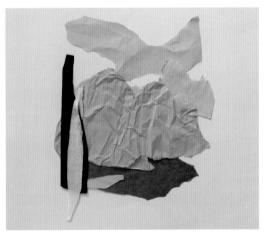

16 Place the 2 long black and white pieces on the left. Overlap the black piece by the white piece to form the waterfall running down from the mountains.

17 Place the 3 dark grey mountains on the collage.

18 Place the grass green mountain on the top left.

19 Place the river components on the lower part of the collage. Be sure to create the flowing effect of the meander.

20 Tear 2 pieces from the dark green embossed paper. Use the crumpling, pinching, and folding techniques to form 3 mountains.

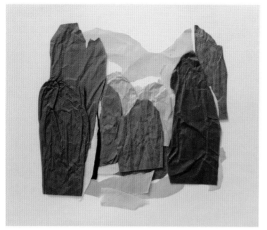

21 Place the 2 dark green mountains on both sides of the collage.

22 Create a few irregular mountains in different sizes from the emerald embossed paper using the crumpling, pinching, and folding techniques.

23 Place the emerald mountains on the right and bottom of the collage.

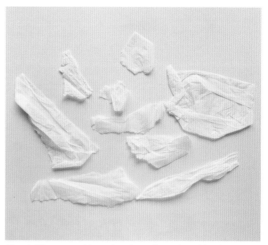

24 Tear several irregular pieces from the white tissue as the clouds.

25 Place the white clouds on the center of the collage, overlapped by the mountain to form the scene of towering into the clouds.

26 Place the rest of the clouds on top of the mountains to form the misty scene. Adjust and set the overall layout.